DEFINITION OF DOWN

My Life with Ice T & the Birth of Hip Hop

Written by Darlene Ortiz & Heidi Cuda

DEFINITION OF DOWN: My Life with Ice T & the Birth of Hip Hop

© 2015 by Darlene Ortiz and Heidi Cuda

Over The Edge Books
Los Angeles, CA
overtheedgebooks.com

ISBN 978-0996423861 - full-color print edition
ISBN 978-1944082994 - electronic edition
ISBN 978-1944082987 - b/w print edition

Design by X Is The Weapon / Cover Photo by Glen E. Friedman

All rights reserved. No part of this book may be reproduced or transmitted in any form or by any means, electronic or mechanical, including photocopying, recording, or by information storage and retrieval systems, without the written permission of the publisher, except by a reviewer who may quote brief passages in a review.

Printed in the United States of America

DEDICATION

To Tracy... with love
To my grandma Connie... for taking me in and giving me love
To my father Pete... my hero
And to Ice... our beautiful son

"Here I am, can I be your fool?
What you want, cuz I'll get it for you?
And I don't know what to do,
Cuz I'm so in love with you,
All my empty pockets spend,
Ride with you til the very end,
Telling you I'm down,
And that I'll do it all again,
That's the definition of down."

by Darlene Ortiz and Teena Marie, from the album *Beautiful*

TABLE OF CONTENTS

	INTRODUCTION	7
1	BABY GIRL	8
2	ROSE	12
3	ESCAPE TO L.A.	20
4	B-GIRL	24
5	ME & T	30
6	MOVIN' ON UP	36
7	THE GAME	54
8	DOPE JAM TOUR	60
9	POWER	64
10	MAKIN' MOVIES & A BABY	82
11	THERE GOES THE NEIGHBORHOOD	92
12	DRAMA	104
13	99 PROBLEMS & D AIN'T ONE	110
14	THE RAIN	118
15	DEFINITION OF DOWN	126
	POSTSCRIPT	138

INTRODUCTION

Looking back at all the photos, articles and home movies of me and Tracy, I see two of the happiest people. In every photo, we're smiling. The love and support, the trust we shared, it seemed like nothing would ever come between us. Ours was a true love story. That we met at the birth of this great cultural revolution known as Hip Hop was no accident. It was in the cards from day one.

Lemme tell you how deep this was. I remember days where we were so hungry, we'd have to conjure up a way to get a meal. He was trying to go legit, get his music out to the world, and there were nights when we simply didn't eat. But we were so happy. Because isn't that what love is? A shared sacrifice of two people reaching for something together. We knew it was a long shot, but it didn't matter how it turned out. I had his back no matter what.

I saw beauty in the struggle. I'd been struggling my whole life and loving him was easy. He made it easy. The world would get to know him as the controversial rap icon Ice T. But to me he was Tracy, a loving, sweet, caring, tender man, who told me he'd take care of me forever. And I believed him.

I BABY GIRL

To understand how a rapper with no label, no money and no car could sweep me off my feet at the age of 17, you have to know what I was running from. I was running from Rose. I was running from a childhood that was alternately happy when I was with my dad's family and terrifying when I was with my mother, Rose.

I was born the fourth daughter to an alcoholic mom, who had a habit of abandoning her children at birth. Unfortunately, we didn't stay abandoned. She'd come collect us once we were toddlers, around the age of three, when we were less work for her. And then the hell would begin.

But those first three years of my life I was surrounded by love. The day I was born, my mother had already given me up, and I was shipped off to the adoption unit. A family member got wind of the adoption and frantically called my dad, Pete. He didn't know she'd gone into labor that day because he and Rose had broken up, and he immediately rushed to the hospital and claimed me as his own.

I was brought into a home in Corona in Riverside County, a suburb surrounded by orange groves about an hour-and-a-half away from Los Angeles. The home was filled with loving grandparents, aunts and uncles, and my father, was an active service man in the Army who was proud of his baby girl. Everyone tells me stories of those happy first few years with my Ortiz family, a loud, loving, tightknit

DEFINITION OF DOWN

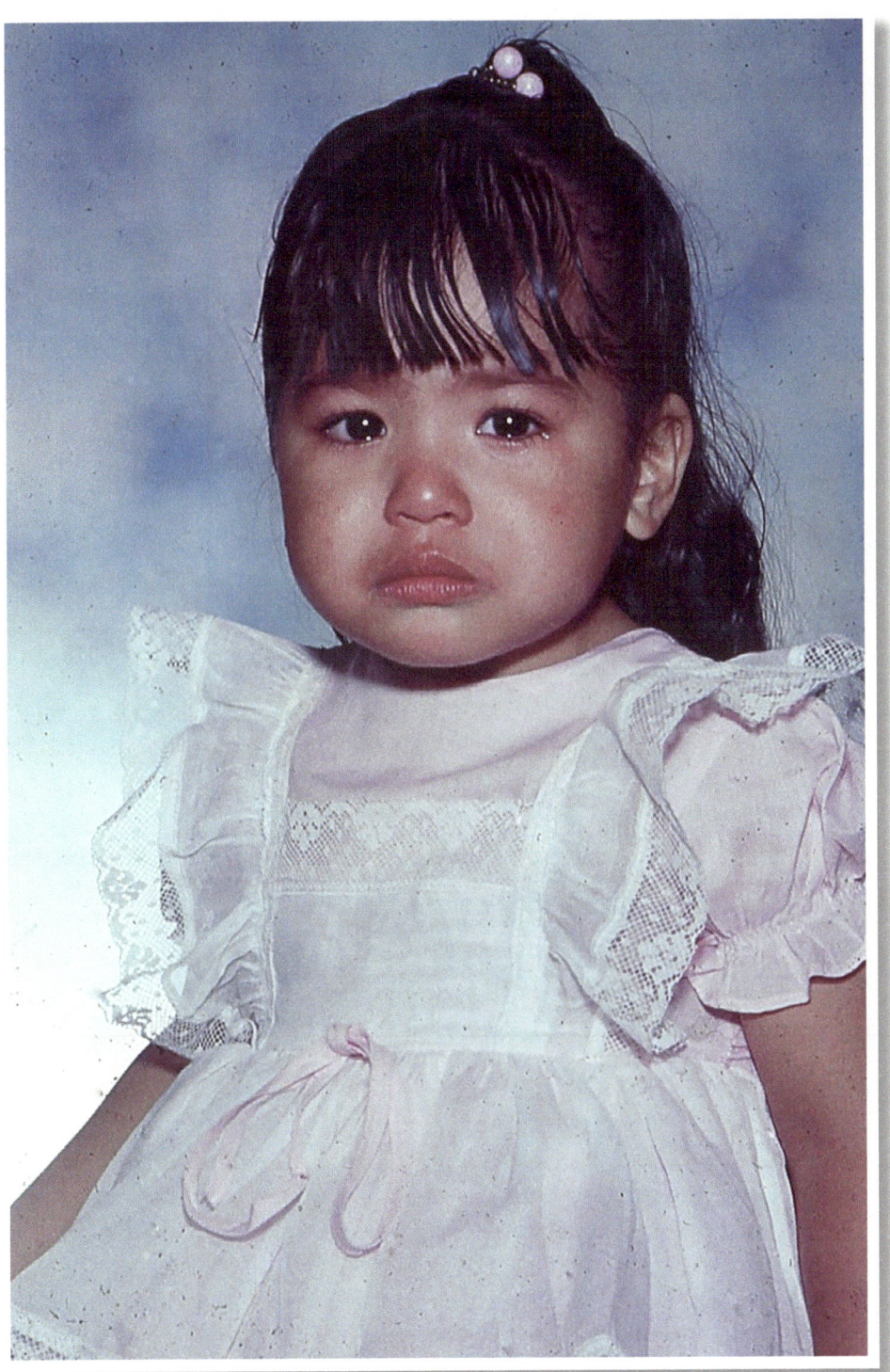

Mexican family. That house, built by the hands of my grandfather, was my safe haven.

By the time I turned three, Pete had begun to have remorse over raising me away from my mother. He knew she had problems, but he thought he could save her–and by doing so, give me a mother. He offered to marry her and to even raise her daughters as his own. And somehow it happened: the ill-fated marriage of Pete and Rose, doomed from the start. But it gave her an opportunity to get her claws in me, and even after they split up two years later, I was forced to live with Rose.

My grandparents' house was 20 minutes away on foot, and I would run there as often as I could. I would show up before school just to get a meal and some love before starting the day. I was the lucky daughter, because I had Pete and I had a real family.

Pete was so cool, a true original. He was a biker, who raised me to be self-sufficient. He'd teach me to fish and how to shoot firearms. I even participated in an Ortiz ritual, witnessing the slaughtering of a pig, where an uncle decreed: "Now, you're an Ortiz!"

Although Pete was a man's man, he also had a sensitive side. He'd braid my hair and iron my dresses. He never missed my games or school events. He was always the cool guy riding up on a Harley, wearing his bandana, ripped jeans and leather boots. I was crazy about my dad. Whenever I was with him, I felt safe, strong and confident. And that's what carried me through some of my darkest days.

Despite having a great job at a steel mill in Fontana, in those days fathers simply weren't awarded custody. Especially ones who looked like my dad. I started running away before kindergarten. Police even found me on the freeway once, trying to take a shortcut to my grandparents' house. Didn't matter. They always returned me to Rose, back to the scene of the crime. Apparently, they had bigger problems to deal with instead of concerning themselves with a young Mexican girl and her alcoholic mother.

DEFINITION OF DOWN

Throughout my childhood, this would become a pattern, where my sisters and I would do anything we could to escape Rose, but we were always sent back because that's just how things were in those days. My closest sister continually went to the police to report abuse, but their pat line was, "If she didn't draw blood, there's nothing we can do." So one day, Rose smacked me so hard with a pillow my nose started to bleed, and my sister took off and came back with two cops. She said, "There you go! There's your proof!" And Rose played it off, putting it back on us, calling it "horseplay." And the two cops bought it. Either that or they just couldn't be bothered, again.

Mothers were supposed to know best, to protect you and love you. Rose didn't exactly have the motherly instinct. She was one cold piece.

# 2 ROSE

So let's start with the good memories of Rose. She made a terrific pineapple upside-down cake. I know I had it more than once. And one time, when I had a prom date pick me up, she didn't ruin it. She even took a couple of pictures and was polite. Might've even been wearing a bra.

But that's where the good times end. Rose was bad to the bone. She was diabolical. She had four daughters by three different men, and only my father tried to step up and make an honest woman out of her. I used to look at this one photo of her, and I could see that she'd once been a beautiful woman. She had perfect skin and that classic model beauty mark made famous by Marilyn Monroe. She was wearing a one-piece bathing suit and looked like a Latina Bettie Page, with a full busty figure and black pinup hair. She had confidence and strength in that faded Polaroid.

I used to stare at that photo and wonder, "What happened to you, Rosie? What made you so mean?" She never talked about her childhood, but I know she was the oldest of 11 kids, and by 15 was a parent of her own. Nobody ever talked about that.

It was a game of survival in Rose's home. We lived in a two-bedroom apartment on a quiet street in Corona. I can still hear her snapping her gum, making disparaging remarks while nursing her Boone's Farm wine. The refrigerator would be empty, but there was always plenty of alcohol. Till this day, I don't know how I made it to school each morning, how I got myself ready. There was no one to wake you up, make you breakfast, pack you a lunch, see you off to school with clean clothes and a smile. But each day, I'd somehow do it on my own, and often in time to get to my grandma's first.

A couple of things I can credit to Rose. She was crazy about posture. She'd smack the shit out of us from behind to force us to stand up straight and we did. Till this day, I have excellent posture. Thanks, Rose. And her other obsession was she was adamant none of us came home pregnant. Not because of any concern for our well-being, but because she made it clear: "I ain't taking care of no fucking kids." She didn't want us, and she surely didn't want any grandchildren.

My friends used to joke about how I could go anywhere and do anything, because Rose didn't care where I went. My friends would literally come over just to witness Rose's response to me asking her permission to go out. You'd hear a voice from upstairs respond, "Are you kidding me? You're waking me for this shit? Hell's Bells! Go ahead, and shut the motherfucker down for all I care." Those became some of the legendary "Rose phrases" my friends and I would use through the years and still till this day.

Everyone thought I was so lucky because Rose was so lenient, but I wanted a mother like they had, who'd say: "Where are you going? Who are you going with? What time does it end? I want you home by midnight."

Looking back, I realize just how notorious Rose was. I was present for her first D.U.I. I was around 12 years old and Rose was driving my sister and I home from my father's house. It was so cold and rainy I grabbed my dad's Army coat as I ran out the door. My sister immediately started arguing with Rose, because she was driving erratically. My sister called her out: "You're drunk!" she said. Rose slurred back, "Ahhh, mind your own business," as we swerved along a two-lane highway.

And boom, suddenly, we found ourselves off the side of the road down a deep embankment, smacked against a dirt wall. Rose had lost control of the vehicle. My sister slammed her head against the windshield and had blood dripping down her forehead. But that didn't stop her from cursing my mom out, snatching me out of the car and running away down the highway.

We realized quickly we were in the middle of nowhere, on a cold and stormy night. This was pre-cell phone, and we had no choice but to go back to the car and wait it out. Rose was semiconscious, moaning incoherently. It took about an hour before my sister was able to flag down a car, and the driver went ahead and contacted the police. As soon as they showed up, my sister demanded that they arrest Rose. She told them she was drunk and had endangered our lives, and they went to the car to get her out.

She came to life when they put the cuffs on her, and she started screaming: "You better not touch my daughters!" There she was, trying to sound like a responsible mom, but it was so ass backwards because she was the one who damn near killed us.

What I didn't know, while I was waiting at the police station for my dad to come get me, was the jacket I had on was loaded with his weed stash. As I sat there, surrounded by officers who finally seemed to get the gravity of our situation, I began to smell a familiar odor. Sniff sniff. Where was it coming from? It was the comforting smell of my daddy. I never smoked weed because my dad was adamant his baby girl would stay away from all drugs, but I sure knew the smell. Then I started looking in the pockets and sho' nuff, his top pocket was loaded with a baggy of skunk weed. I nudged my sister and pointed to the pocket. She came closer and sniffed it, and her eyes got big. "Oh shit!" she whispered.

So there I was, my mother's in jail, and I'm in possession. My father comes running in to the police station, quickly thanks the cops, and then he rushed us the hell out of there. We got in his car, and we immediately traded jackets. And that's when we all started laughing. It was all so crazy that we couldn't help but laugh.

My sister was finally vindicated because Rose was where she

needed to be. Locked up. Unfortunately, they let her out.

* * * * * *

Every day was drama with Rose. She just never let up. I look back now, and I can appreciate the macabre humor. And I see how I was actually in training to be the perfect gangsta wife. Nothing shocked me.

According to the National Children's Alliance, nearly 700,000 children are abused or neglected annually, and more than three million children received preventive services from Child Protective Services in 2011. But back in the '70s, when I was coming up, turning a blind eye to abused children was pretty commonplace, even within families. I look back and I wonder where Rose's family was in all this, all those brothers and sisters, they knew what was up but no one intervened.

Rose could turn on the charm when the officers showed up at our door. She had an amazing green thumb and the patio always looked so lush and well tended. Whenever officers showed up at our door, she could always play it off. Our home was always clean; nothing ever out of place, and the cops would just shrug and walk away. And when you've been repeatedly let down year after year by the authorities that are supposed to protect you, you might just decide to take matters into your own hands. I felt it was the only way I could save myself.

I had taken her pinching, shoving, squeezing and verbal abuse year after year. Even as a little girl, I thought to myself, "That's just Rose. What can I do?" It's just the way things were. One of my sisters fought back all the time, and did her best to protect me, but I just took it in stride. Until the day she went too far.

I was 13 and there were no other sisters left in the house. Rose occasionally disappeared for days at a time. One day, I took the opportunity to have a male friend over, and we were watching TV when suddenly I heard Rose coming up through the patio gate. She never wanted anyone in the house, and I told my friend to hurry up and hide and not to make a sound. I got up to meet Rose at the door, and she was clearly on a bender. She was stinking drunk, and we've already established that Rose was a mean drunk. She was going off on my dad, telling me how she'd gone to his house and he'd asked her to leave. She turned her anger on me, and with fire in her eyes, she raged: "And you look just like him!"

And like Frankenstein, with arms outstretched and two clawed hands, she came right at me and wrapped those hands around my throat. And we went down. I can still see vivid details in my head, the dark blue color of the carpet, the dusty ceiling and the front door wide open. I remember the coldness as I hit the ground, how I was trying to gasp for air and wondering what my friend was doing and thinking, hiding somewhere while this scene was playing itself out.

As she's choking me, she's telling me that I'll never see my family again, that I'll never see my father again, that she's gonna move away, and I'm literally terrified not only for my life but for what my life might be if I live. And then, she heard a noise.

She jumped up, releasing her hands off my throat, and found my friend cowering in the living room in a corner behind a wicker wall hanging. As soon as he saw her coming toward him, he made like a bat out of hell, my hell, leaving me alone to deal with my mother. Without skipping a beat, Rose came back toward me, her rage and threats continuing, as she made her way to her room to pass out.

With welts visible on my neck and a growing pain each time I swallowed, I went to my room and started to really think about what she'd said and what she'd done. Yes, she could have killed me that day. That much was clear. I knew my friend, despite his cowardice, had saved my life just by being present. But I knew in my heart that Rose meant what she said, and she was going to ruin the rest of my life.

So I made up my mind. That was the last time she was ever gonna put her hands on me. I was gonna show her. I waited in my room for hours trying to come up with a plan, I was so desperate. The thought of never seeing my father and grandparents again was more than I could bear. Rose wasn't one to make idle threats. Finally, a plan started to formulate. I was going to make it look like an accident. Rose was always falling asleep with a cigarette, and I figured it was only a matter of time before she lit her bed on fire. I was simply going to expedite the process.

It took hours for me to creep to her room. I'd take a step and then wait, and then another, and I'd wait. I brought a baseball bat for protection in case she woke up. Finally, I summoned the courage to enter her room. She was passed out drunk, the ashtray overflowing next to her bed. I stood there for the longest time, looking at her with disgust as sweat rolled down my face.

It was nearly dawn when I finally took her lighter off the nightstand. I reached under her bed and flicked the flame and waved it under the mattress, holding it until I smelled smoke. I started to go into shock because I realized I'd actually done it. Rose began to moan, waking up and coming to. I had the baseball bat, and as I started to swing, I realized what I was doing was wrong and would likely ruin the rest of my life.

The bat limply went down and collided with her head, not a crack or a thunk, but enough to draw blood and wake her up completely. She shot up in bed, holding her head, and looked at me with a horror I'd never seen. It was probably a look she'd seen on my face plenty of times, but I'd never seen it on hers. As much as I hated Rose, I knew I couldn't go through with it and had to help her. She actually looked pathetic in that moment.

"Your bed's on fire!" I screamed. Quickly, we both grabbed the mattress and pulled it to the floor and took the burning box springs and tossed it out of her balcony window onto the patio where it continued to burn. A neighbor called the fire department, and they quickly showed up. And so did the fire chief, who just happened to be my best friend's father. He knew there were problems in my home, and he took one look around and asked my mom to explain what happened. While the paramedics were cleaning up her forehead, she was looking directly at me. And I was looking directly back at her. My eyes said: "You're never gonna hurt me again." I didn't know how long I was going away, but I made it clear to her no matter what it took, she wasn't going to ever lay a hand on me ever again.

That's when Rose took the fall. She started to tell a story about how she fell asleep, and her bed caught on fire from the cigarette, how she got up and started to run down the stairs, and how she tripped and fell and hit her head on the corner of a cabinet. The fire chief looked at me and looked back at her. He knew she was lying. I know he knew. And suddenly, everything changed.

I looked at Rose and said, "I'm going to Grandma's."

She didn't respond. I walked out the door, I looked back at her, and I could see a sadness in her. She knew she'd been defeated. She would no longer be able to control me with her fists and with fear. And from that moment on, Rose never laid a hand on me again.

DEFINITION OF DOWN

3 ESCAPE TO L.A.

I still lived with Rose. She was surviving off my child support and there was no way she'd let me move out. But I was rarely home. I immersed myself in sports: softball, basketball and track. I was active year round and the best part about it was Rose never came to a single game. But Pete showed up, cheering me on while all the girls looked on admiringly.

And he made sure to keep the boys in check. By junior high, I'd already developed, and long before anyone ever heard the phrase "baby got back," I had become locally famous for the junk in my trunk.

Boys used to come up behind me and pretend to be warming their hands like my ass was on fire. They weren't used to seeing Latinas with so much fullness and thick legs. When I played catcher, boys used to gather behind the plate and whoop it up. But Pete would give them that look, and they would ease off. I loved it.

I used to rock yellow Dittos, the tighter the better, with Hawaiian print Vans that I'd custom make from a shop in Orange County. Today, asses like mine have been popularized and women are doing crazy things to get that look; but back then, girls would stick their nose up at me and say, "Omigawd, like, that ain't cute."

So, in the words of Too Short, I decided to get in where I fit in, and I ventured out of my neighborhood and became an accidental tourist on R&B night at a nearby skate rink, where it was predominantly a black crowd. I swear the heavens parted when I walked in, and I could hear, "Ooooh, shoot! Check this girl out!"

I had found my scene. I may have been a young Mexican teenage girl, but I was embraced by the folks at that rink. I watched everyone strut their moves, dancing, cutting loose, and it blew my mind.

Soon as I hit the floor, all eyes turned toward me. I'll never forget what was playing at that moment. It was backwards skate time and Skyy's "Call Me" came over the speakers. This young brother with a Jheri curl, wearing pleated jeans and a mesh shirt, was skating and pantomiming the lyrics to me: "Call me if you need someone to talk to! Call me, satisfaction guaranteed."

At first, I didn't know what the deal was. I was getting more attention than I'd ever received anywhere else, but I couldn't tell if it was for real. Back then, things were very segregated, and I'd never had the opportunity to mix with other cultures. I quickly realized it was for real. I felt so embraced, like the people in this scene really wanted me to be there.

It wasn't just my looks, it was my love for the music. I could skate, I could dance, I felt like Cinderella had arrived at the ball. I started going there every week, and right away, I began dating outside my race. It scandalized my school. Cholitas would come up to me and say, "Eyyyyy, we hear you're starting to go out with black guys? What's that like?" I would tell them it was cool.

I'd had boyfriends since I was 12 years old. My first boyfriend used to pick me up in his lowrider with hops. When I started dating black teens, we'd head straight to the hottest house parties. That's when Hip Hop was just making its way west, and I fell in love with everything about the b-boy scene: the colors, the vibrancy, the fashion, but mostly the moves.

I learned how to uprock and pop lock, I learned ticking and freaking. To appease the older folks in the scene, I learned how to do a mean chacha, not the classic version but the street version. I was so into the scene, I had a graffiti artist come to my home and cover every inch of my room. I became a b-girl, and I didn't realize it at the time, but this would be my ticket out. Before long, I would escape to L.A.

4 B-GIRL

Corona was about to get a seismic shift of cool in the form of two Puerto Rican cousins who moved from Brooklyn: Nereida and Lourdes. As soon as they landed at my school, people were talking about them, doing the small town thing. But I went right up to both of them and said, "I like your style."

They were head-to-toe in "Flashdance" cool, with early Madonna sprinkled in. They had the headbands, the off-the-shoulder sweatshirts, genie pants and fingerless gloves. And boy could they dance. We instantly formed a crew called the Heartbreakers.

We started entering dance contests that took us to different cities, where we linked up with other dancers and you could feel the energy of this movement. There was such a buzz, and we were a part of it. I would hitch a ride to L.A. every chance I got to compete in this new scene. One of the benefits of being Rose's daughter is she didn't care where I was or what I was doing.

I looked upon this as an opportunity. I entered as many contests as possible, and one night in Pomona, when I was dancing with my crew in a big competition, one of the judge's started flirting with me. My crew won the competition that night, and I left with the judge's number. His name was Oz Rock.

He'd already made a name for himself in the breakdancing world, doing commercials and representing the true b-boy culture.

DEFINITION OF DOWN

He came from the East Coast and quickly became famous in L.A. for being one of the first to demonstrate windmills and head-spins, some of the more difficult moves. He was gorgeous, a powerful, buffed dancer of Cuban descent who preferred hitting the floor in speedos.

He was a pioneer of the scene, and I was awestruck. The Heartbreakers and I were so excited to get to meet this phenomenon in person. The fact that I went home with his number was a very big deal in my crew.

He was a rock star in the dance world, and when he came to my high school to pick me up for our first date, it was like a scene out of *Breakin'*.

He was dressed in a polo shirt and sweatpants and his ubiquitous headband. People gathered around his car to meet him, and he loved putting on a show for a crowd. He'd dance for anyone, even when we were driving through town. We'd hit a red light, and he'd jump out of the car and climb up on the roof and start doing windmills, spinning like a crazy top on his back. He was so fast. People would start to honk, but not because they wanted him to move his car, but in support of his performance.

The first thing he asked me when we started dating was, "Have you been to Radiotron?" I'd never been but I dreamed about going. It was mecca for the dance scene, and everyone talked about it. It became nationally famous because it's where they shot the two *Breakin'* movies. It was a youth center in the MacArthur Park area of L.A., and it transformed into an all-ages dance club at night. Radiotron had its roots in an underground club called Radio that formed in 1980 before being shut down. Out of its ashes came Radiotron, which was the heartbeat of L.A.'s b-boy scene.

Oz Rock took me there on our first date, and I was sprung from day one. It was like walking onto the set of *Breakin'* with the graffiti'd entrance and the music thumpin'. As I looked around I saw people from every race and background, from young kids to dancers in their

20s. It was just so cool. Radiotron became my home, literally. I used to sleep there!

I met the youth center director, Carmello Alvarez. He was a surrogate father to everyone in the scene and that included me. I started going there regularly, and I'd hitch a ride from anyone heading into L.A. As soon as I'd see the downtown skyline, I'd light up because I was meant for the big city. And for me, that meant Radiotron.

I wouldn't always have a ride home, and Carmello would invite me to stay in his office if I didn't have a place to go. You could lock the door from the inside, and he always made sure I was safe. Sometimes I'd stay there with Oz Rock, and other dancers would crash there as well.

Oz was getting so much commercial work, he started traveling a lot. At one point, he took off for the Philippines and word got back to me he'd knocked up a local girl there. I broke it off as soon as I heard, and I started going to Radiotron solo.

And that's when I met Tracy.

DEFINITION OF DOWN

5 ME & T

I was 17, and I needed a ride to Radiotron. I was still living with Rose, but we steered clear of each other. I retreated to my world, and she lived in hers. I had no car and no license but I had to get out of that house as often as possible, and Radiotron was the perfect escape.

One Friday night in 1985, I called up a friend who had wheels. He was a handsome Latino, whose family owned a local dairy farm. He agreed to drive me to L.A. in his Porsche, and we arrived in style. MacArthur Park in those days was sketchy, and we found a spot right in front of the club. It was around Christmas, and lights were twinkling everywhere. The streets were lined with tinsel and light-up candy canes, and Santas were out panning for cash.

I remember everything about that night. I was wearing a grey pleather skirt, with black lace tights and Converse. By then, I was nicknamed Glamorous D by the Radiotron regulars, and as soon as I arrived, my buddy Jazzy D passed me the mic. You can still find the video of me on YouTube rapping: "Break dance, coast to coast, it's the thing we like to do the most..." My wide belt was slung low, my big permed hair adding about six inches to my height, glitter everywhere.

I never sought out rapping, but as part of the Radiotron scene, we did a little bit of everything. Looking at that clip from '84, I look so dang happy. It was so fun to be on that stage, like we were all stars. I moved onto the dance floor and started doing my thing to "Renegades of Funk" by Afrika Bambaataa, when all of a sudden the music came to a stop and we looked up and saw a group hopping up on the stage. They were wearing real leather pants and the guy with the mic had on a fedora.

The audience started whispering, "Hey! That's the rapper from the *Breakin'* movies!" I was mesmerized by his voice and his presence. He was the flyest guy I'd ever seen. He had moves and style. He was wearing leather gloves and a studded belt, with Porsche Carrera sunglasses.

When his set ended, I just wanted to get right back on the dance floor. My friend Animation, another Radiotron regular, started making his way across the dance floor to me. He was pointing behind him, like he was warning me. When he reached me he whispered, "That guy, Ice T, wanted me to come over here and tell you he wants to talk to you. I just want to warn you, these aren't the kind of guys you're used to."

I asked him, "What does he want to talk to me about?" Animation said, "He's got an album coming out soon, and he wants you to be on the cover." Even at 17, I knew that was a line. But that's when my date, the dairy boy, said: "You should go talk to him! Could be a good opportunity."

I rolled my eyes because I couldn't figure out what was worse: staying on this side of the dance floor with naive dairy boy or going over to the other side of the dance floor to talk to the leather-clad rapper with the hustle.

I looked over at the rapper and saw this big grin, and for the first time I noticed his dimples. And then I noticed his hazel eyes. By the time I made my way to him, he was holding court with a group of young fans. I watched how he talked to these kids, inspiring them and making them laugh. I could tell they looked up to him. He turned his attention to me and started pouring on the compliments.

"Girl, your eyes are so beautiful... look at that smile..."

He was really pouring it on. He invited me to have a seat. I remember how everyone was watching us from afar. He started asking about me and about my life. When I started to tell him my age, he said, "Stop! Oh, hell no!"

Before he could get too worked up, I told him I was just about to turn 18, and he looked very relieved. He told me he'd just wrecked his car and had no wheels, and when I told him I lived in Corona, a solid two hours from L.A., he was bummed. Back then, Riverside County was a world away.

He told me he had a girl living with him, but even though the relationship was over, he didn't want to put her out on the street. He was up front about everything, and I wasn't used to men speaking so honestly. He was looking straight into my eyes, and he kept saying, "Man, I'm really feelin' you."

He asked if he could have my number, and when we went to exchange numbers, he told me he didn't have a phone. So I'm thinking, no wheels, no phone and a girlfriend. Kinda sketchy. But he was so charming, and there was something about his honesty that really felt right. By the time we said goodbye, my ride had left, pissed off, and I didn't even care. I hitched a ride home with another dancer, and I thought about Tracy the entire ride back. I was shocked when he called the next day. He wasn't playin'.

Unfortunately, Rose got to the phone first. I was horrified, listening to her giving him the third degree. She finally yells up to me, "Darlene, sounds like a grown ass man calling for you!" I ran to the phone. And from then on, we spent hours at a time getting to know each other over Pac Bell.

He was calling me from a pay phone at the top of Beachwood Canyon in Hollywood. He apologized because every few minutes we'd be interrupted by the operator asking for more change, but he

DEFINITION OF DOWN

always had plenty of coins.

We made a plan for him to come visit. As luck should have it, his manager lived in Riverside, so we set a date to meet at his house. The big event was set for the next Friday.

Tracy took a Greyhound bus from L.A. People might find it hard believe that Ice T would ride public transportation, but back then, there was no shame in his game. The entire day at school, I couldn't concentrate on anything else. I kept waiting for the clock to strike 3 pm. When it finally came, I begged a girlfriend to drive me to Riverside and hang out for awhile.

I didn't even have to look for the street address because there were kids gathered around his manager's house, peering in the window, trying to see Tracy. I don't know if they recognized him from *Breakin'* or if it was just his magnetism, but he always seemed to draw people toward him, even back then.

He was waiting for me at the door. I took one look at him and wanted to jump his bones. He offered to take me on a tour of the house, and I thought that was a line. I was preparing for you-know-what, but he actually took me on a tour of the house. The irony is, he wanted to take things nice and slow.

As unbelievable as it may sound, he wanted to meet my family first. I was shocked. I figured he'd just want to get me alone, but he was the total opposite of what people would assume. There was no way I was taking him home to Rose, that thought didn't even cross my mind. So I told him everyone in the Ortiz family would be at my aunt's house, and he said: "Let's roll!" My girlfriend drove us to my aunt's home in Corona and dropped us off. And the moment he walked in the door, he turned it on and charmed my entire family.

Oh, and he could be so charming. We still have photos of him holding my pregnant aunt's stomach and posing with my cousins.

DEFINITION OF DOWN

My family ordered pizza, and he insisted on paying. That may sound like a small thing, but for my family, it was a really big deal. Little did they know how generous he would be as his fame exploded. But on that night, that small token will always be remembered as very special.

Everyone was impressed by him. They knew how excited I was that he was coming to visit, and before he left, they gave me the thumbs up. His manager came to pick him up, and that was the beginning of the next 17 years of my life.

6 MOVIN' ON UP

"I hear you're seeing this guy," said Pete. "Everyone's talking about him." That was my dad, checking up on his girl.

"Does he treat you well?" he asked. I told him he did.

"Are you happy?" I told him I was.

And that was it. If I was happy, Pete was happy.

Rose, on the other hand, wasn't happy. Not just because he was black. She made it clear she didn't approve of that. And not just because he was older, at 26. But because she saw the day coming when I was going to leave, and with that, she would no longer be able to use me to bankroll her.

She'd call him names, refer to him as an albino and call him ugly. I'd just look at her like she was crazy. She'd never met him; she was just basing her opinions on secondhand information.

But really, what she was doing was playing dirty pool, trying to turn me against him so she wouldn't lose child support.

Even though I knew she was nuts, she did have one thing right: I was on my way out that door. Tracy and I continued to talk on the phone as often as possible. He must've robbed a laundromat because he never ran out of quarters.

DEFINITION OF DOWN

It was becoming painfully obvious it was time for me to move on, and I came up with a plan. I had family living in Orange County, and I decided to continue my high school studies there since that was one county closer to Tracy.

* * * * * *

Just after my 18th birthday, "it" went down. It went down in a Comfort Inn in Anaheim, Room 12, with Tracy cruising down to the O.C. in a borrowed car. Although I'm not much to kiss and tell, I will say this: if that vanity mirror could talk, it would be blushing right about now. I thought I knew what time it was, but it was kid stuff compared to what Tracy exposed me to. I realized, "Oh, this is what people are talking about." Having a man nine years older than me had certain advantages.

You have to figure, the romance had been building for months. People don't think twice to make a phone call now, but each night he was walking to a pay phone, standing out in the cold, spending hours at a time on the phone with his girl. So that night in his arms was S-P-E-C-T-A-C-U-L-A-R. Tracy was such a romantic. The words he used were so sweet, and he made me feel so beautiful, like I was the only girl in the world. And for years, I was. In his arms that night, we knew we had to be together from then on. By then, his ex-girlfriend had moved out, and I asked him if I could move in with him.

He was surprised because I was still in high school, and he was living in a converted garage, barely a single and totally illegal. There was no kitchen, only a plug-in hot plate, and hardly enough room for one person, let alone two. The only furniture was a water bed and a busted up old couch.

But Tracy said yes, I could move in with him. And what others might have thought was a dingy shack was a castle to me, and I was its princess. It was on a famous street in the Hollywood Hills in Beachwood Canyon, right under the Hollywood sign. I was so excited because we were in Hollywood! And it was our love shack.

I finished high school at Hollywood High Adult School, while Tracy worked on his music. We were so broke. He'd left behind a life of crime, determined to make his mark as a rapper. And rhyme wasn't paying, yet.

One day, I was sunbathing and the only thing I could scrounge up was Crisco. Go ahead and laugh, but I'm telling you we were flat busted. I told Tracy the only downside was it was really hard to wash off. He disappeared for a few minutes and came back with a surprise.

"I told you I would never go back to a life of crime again," he said. "But I had to get you this."

And out from his pocket came a bottle of Bain de Soleil, the hottest and most expensive suntan oil in the '80s. I knew he didn't have a dime in his pocket and he stole that bottle, and I'm pretty sure it was the last crime he committed, but I was so moved. I kept that bottle for years.

Every day, it was me and him against the world.

He used to get so frustrated that we didn't have more, and he'd always say: "One day, baby, we're gonna have it all."

In my mind, I already did.

* * * * * *

I would've done anything for him. I was so in love. I finished high school, and I knew I had to get a job ASAP.

He was determined to stay away from any illegal ways of making money, because he knew the end wouldn't justify the means. His friends were still caught up in that world, but they would do everything they could to keep him out of it.

DEFINITION OF DOWN

He'd gotten his first taste of legit money when he worked on *Breakin'*, and he didn't want to blow his shot at fame by going back to a life of crime. He saw where that got some of his homeboys, basically dead or in prison. He knew he had a true chance at making it and so did his friends, who despite what they may have been doing, really did support him in his efforts to go legit.

During this time, I was the definition of down. I knew he had the dream of making it as a rapper, and I knew he had what it took. But it didn't matter to me one way or the other. I was happy just being by his side. I had no problem being the one to support us financially. He'd work on his beats during the day, while I went off to work.

I'd gotten lucky because I met a woman at a graffiti exhibit who owned a popular restaurant in Santa Monica called Charmer's French Market. She introduced herself to us at the art show by telling me how much she loved my look and would I be interested in a job. Tracy and I both looked at each other and said: "Yup! She'll take it!" That's exactly what I needed! I was wearing a zebra-print

jumpsuit and white thigh-high leather boots with five inch heels and sporting a two-toned faux hawk.

She told me I'd make a perfect hostess for her restaurant. We were shocked! We needed money, and since I'd never worked before I had no idea how to go out and get a job. This one was handed to me. I asked her what the requirements were and she said: "Just be yourself."

She said the restaurant was being remodeled and wouldn't open for another couple of months, but she immediately made her boyfriend hire me to work at his art gallery in the meantime.

I went home that night knowing I had a job come Monday morning. I couldn't believe it! We both felt it was the beginning of things going our way. That Monday, I became the receptionist for a gallery on Melrose Avenue, a trendy hotspot in Hollywood. I opened the place in the morning and did whatever needed to be done. Everything was going great until I started letting the homies come in. Among them was Fab Five Freddy, who was doing art for the gallery. He'd ask to use the phone and I let him, but unknown to me, he was calling New York and would gab for hours. I walked into the office one morning, and there he was, feet on the owner's desk, yacking away, and when I went to close up at night, he was still yacking away.

DEFINITION OF DOWN

No one had cell phones back in the day and even I took the opportunity to call my grandmother in Riverside periodically.

When the bill showed up about a month later, boy, was I in for a surprise. The owner flipped out and that was the end of my art gallery days. Till this day, Fab Five Freddy and I laugh about it, and he always takes the blame for getting me fired.

The timing was perfect for my firing because Charmer's was just reopening, and I made my debut as a hostess. It was awesome! It was *the* spot for Hollywood's old money crowd. Johnny Carson was a regular, and he loved Charmer's because no one made a fuss over him. He was treated like just another guest, even though my heart would skip a beat every time I seated him.

Charmer's was just like it sounds, a charming French-themed marketplace with a restaurant that turned into a clubby atmosphere at night with music and DJs. Even though I was taking three buses to get there and three to get home late at night, I loved supporting Tracy's dream. He was working on his music full-time and my paycheck helped us scrape by.

One night I was coming home late, and as I was getting ready to transfer buses, a desperate dude came out of nowhere and tried to snatch my purse. People on the bus started yelling at the thief, who got spooked and ran off without my bag. The incident bothered Tracy, and he decided I was no longer taking buses to work.

We'd scraped together enough cash to get his old Porsche running. It was the one he'd wrecked before we met and we had just enough to get it on the streets, but boy, was it illegal. First off, I didn't have a driver's license. Secondly, he'd chopped the top off so it didn't have a roof, and instead of headlights it had two gaping holes. It didn't have heat or a radio, not even any interior paneling. It was primer gray and looked like I'd stolen it from a chop shop. But it was my ride.

One night, I was driving home from the restaurant, and it was raining

outside. I promised Tracy I wouldn't take the freeway, and I was shivering down a surface street on my way to Beachwood Canyon where we lived. On the side of the road, I could see two police officers getting ready to make an arrest, and everyone turned to look at me and you could see their jaws drop, including the would-be criminals.

The cops immediately came after me instead. I pulled over and one of them said to me: "Are you serious? Where do I start? There are so many violations here. Okay, let's see your license and registration."

Oops.

He looked at my sorry ass and just shook his head. He told me, "Just go home." There was so much wrong shit he didn't want to deal with me. I made it to Beachwood that night, and Tracy decided it was a sign that I needed a job that was closer to home.

And I got one. Tracy had his manager fake me a resume with a stellar recommendation as a secretarial ace, and I got hired to work as a head receptionist for a real estate company. On my first day, the woman who hired me took me into her office and said, "You know

DEFINITION OF DOWN

I know that resume was bogus." I didn't breathe. Then she said, "But I like you kid. Welcome."

So there I was, a junior exec jumping on the Number 1 bus to my downtown job, happy as can be. Tracy may have been legit, grinding away on his beats all day, but he still had plenty of hustle.

I came home from work one night and he had that look in his eye that told me he was up to something. He had a big grin on his face and said, "Baby, I got a plan for easy money." I was so tired, but he knew I'd do anything for him and we surely did need cash.

He said, "You still got that purple leatherette thong?"

I said, "You know this."

He said, "Egyptian Lover is having a dance contest for 'I Need a Freak.'" Egyptian Lover was a hot dance artist at that time and the contest was for his new single.

Tracy was convinced I could easily make it to the top 5, and he had devised a scheme that would take me to number 1. So junior exec morphed into an exotic dancer that night. Just like Tracy said, I made it to the top 5 with my dance moves. But when it came down to the final dance, I got up there, peeled off my mini skirt to reveal that purple leatherette thong with the black lace and silver studs, and the crowd went wild.

We celebrated all the way home in our janky-ass Porsche, a thousand dollars richer and a bouquet of roses in my hands.

Grinning from ear to ear, Tracy said: "I told ya!"

So did we take that cash and go to Rodeo Drive? No. Did we go to The Ivy and pay for an over-priced meal? No. The very next morning, we got up extra early and bought... chairs.

We'd never had chairs at our love shack, just milk crates covered with towels. He had a poster of the "Blown-Away Man," the famous ad for Hitachi Maxell where a guy sitting in a leather chair gets wind-blown by his speakers. Tracy loved those Le Corbusier chairs, and we took our cash and headed straight for East Hollywood where we got the best pair of fake Le Corbusier chairs money could buy.

And on that day, I witnessed the birth of "Antoine."

Tracy doesn't know who Antoine is because I never told him, but that's my secret alias for his designer alter ego. That day was the first time he ever had enough cash to entertain his inner interior designer, but later when the real money started rolling in, Antoine moved in and took over.

* * * * * *

Little by little, bit by bit, we were starting to do better. I continued to work downtown and support him, and with the help of his friends, we even had a little savings.

One of our favorite free pastimes was to walk down to Hollywood Boulevard on a Saturday afternoon and window shop. Hand in hand, we'd check out all the funky stores like Playmates, a women's clothing boutique that specialized in lingerie and erotic clothing. We'd grab a slice of pizza and split it or on a better night we'd get the rib plate at Chicken Delight.

DEFINITION OF DOWN

We became fixtures on the boulevard and made friends with a lot of the shop owners. I still have the first pair of shoes he ever bought me on one of those outings. They're black leather stiletto pumps, with a pointed toe and four-inch heels. Any time he had any extra cash in his pocket, he'd find something to buy me.

At the time, Hollywood Boulevard was still grimy, and it was excellent people-watching turf. You'd see b-boys, wannabe poseur pimps, '80s hair bands with ripped up shirts and spandex pants. Everyone was a freak and everyone fit in.

One day when we were walking the boulevard, I saw a box on a sidewalk with a little pitbull puppy in it. The owner said he'd been selling them all day, and there was one last pup left. She was a little brindle girl, and it was love at first sight. I knew we couldn't afford it, so I just kept walking past her into a store. I looked for Tracy, but he'd stayed outside. After a few minutes, I went back outside and saw that the guy and the box with the pitbull had left. I looked around for Tracy and saw that in his hands was that little brindle girl.

He said, "D, I've got a surprise for you!" He handed me the puppy and said: "Meet Felony." Oh, man, I loved that little girl so much! That was our first baby. We would have a bunch of dogs in the future with straight up hood names, but that was our first lil pit.

I never asked how much he paid for her, but I'm guessing he emptied his pocket of everything he had just to make me happy. Lil Miss Felony became a loving member of the family but she didn't ingratiate us with the landlords, so we were forced to move out of our little love shack. We made a lateral move to another tiny apartment at Hollywood Boulevard and Franklin Avenue, but this one had a kitchen. Well, not really a kitchen. It had a sink and a stove but no oven. Still, it was an improvement.

The good thing was it took dogs. The bad thing was it was thrashed. Antoine immediately stepped it up. We walked to a nearby hardware store and Antoine bought a gang of black paint. We spent our first night

there painting everything black. I was so in love with him, I thought it was genius. It looked like a nightclub when we were done.

We moved in the old waterbed and our two awesome chairs, a stereo tower and a fatback TV, and that was pretty much all our worldly possessions.

* * * * * *

The day came when he finally finished enough tracks to try to get a record deal, but as hard as he tried to shop it in L.A. no one was buying. Execs would look at him like, "Rap?! Really?" They weren't getting it. Even though wherever you looked, Hip Hop culture was exploding and he had even released his own singles on independent labels, but major labels in L.A. were way behind the times.

He woke up one day and told me he'd made a decision. "D, the only way I'm going to get a record deal is if I go to New York. It just ain't happening here."

As much as I didn't want him to leave, I knew he was right. I could see how frustrated he was not any getting love in L.A.

So we scrounged up the money to get him to New York. It was 1986 and the East Coast had already given us such artists as Grandmaster Flash, Melle Mel & the Furious Five, Run DMC, Beastie Boys, Afrika Bambaataa, Salt-N-Pepa and Whodini. Record labels there had a template for this bold new music style.

DEFINITION OF DOWN

While I was living in L.A. with Felony holding down the fort, Tracy was staying in the Bronx getting to know everyone. The producer he was working with, Afrika Islam, was from the Bronx and Tracy became tight with some of the known rappers.

As I look back, I realize just how brilliant a move it was to go to New York. He was the first L.A. rapper to make the East Coast pilgrimage, and they embraced him.

I was still sending him money and doing what I could to help him, and one day I got a phone call. He'd only been out there for less than two months and he said: "D, I did it."

I was like, "Whaaaat???!!!!"

Truth is, I never had any doubt. He'd set out for New York to get himself a record deal and he did it.

He told me, "Look, D, you better get prepared because you're going to New York!" He told me to give my two-week notice at work. He said, "You're never working again. I'm going to take care of you." He told me to get Felony looked after by family because he was coming for me. We still didn't have any money, and people at work told me I was crazy. They'd say, "That rap thing is just a fad," and they'd look at me with pity.

On my last day of work, Tracy called me and told me he had a surprise for me. At 5 o'clock sharp, I heard a horn honk. We all scrambled to the window to see what was going on. There was Tracy, six floors down, in a bright red BMW 740, waving through the sunroof with a big old smile.

I ran down six flights of stairs, hopped into that car and never looked back.

* * * * * *

We flew straight to New York. It was right around Christmas, and it was freezing cold. I had no proper clothes, and we were staying in the South Bronx. He had just enough money to get us back to New York, and he kept reassuring me a bigger check was coming. The place where we were staying had a communal bathroom down the hall, where a machete hung by the side of the toilet in case any unwanted visitors scampered your way.

Sure enough, four days later that check showed up and we moved into the baller suite at the top floor of the Marriott Hotel in Times Square. We had officially arrived.

Tracy wanted to take me shopping. I have a photo of myself before he took me into Gucci and after I came out.

In the before picture, I'm wearing a tiny little jacket and Reeboks with no socks and you can literally see my goosebumps. After I came out, I'm wearing Gucci riding boots with a matching tote handbag. He bought me a leather and fur jacket that took the chill away. I wasn't even into designer clothes or spending a lot of money on luxury items, and I'm still not, but it made him so happy to take care of his girl.

We must have spent an entire week as conspicuous consumers, going to the Village for leather clothing and Canal Street for custom jewelry. I got a name ring that spelled out Darlene. One of the key pieces from that week was a gold gun pendant that Tracy wore for years. We both wore it on some pretty famous album covers.

I've never been materialistic, it's just not in my nature. Even later on, when Tracy was raking in the big bucks, you'd find me at Slauson Swap Meet in South Central, not Rodeo Drive in Beverly Hills. That was Tracy's thing. He showered me with high-end jewelry and clothes and was proud he was able to provide for me the way he'd always wanted to.

For him, it was all about the game, and that's why I wasn't surprised he could go to New York and within weeks come back with a record deal and enough to buy his first BMW with cash he earned legit. He was a natural-born hustler, a force of nature. When he put his mind

DEFINITION OF DOWN

on something, you best believe it was gonna get handled.

That entire time in New York, we were like two kids on Christmas morning. Only a few months before, we were trying to plot how we were going to eat. Now, we were ordering room service, with shrimps the size of my fist. Tracy could get his ultimate favorite delivered to his door: eggs benedict.

Yes, we were George and Weezy, and we were movin' on up.

7 THE GAME

As I look back at that Christmas we spent on the top of the Marriott overlooking the bright lights of Times Square, it was like a fairy tale, a Hip Hop fairy tale. One night we took a gypsy cab back to the South Bronx to producer Afrika Islam's home, where everyone was meeting up to go clubbin'. All of a sudden, a limo pulls up in front of Islam's tenement and our friends got all excited, talking about this boxing prodigy who was making a name for himself.

This yoked up teenager nicely dressed gets out of the limo and makes his way into Islam's apartment. Everyone's taking pictures and cheering him on, telling him he's gonna be the next big heavyweight champion.

I just remember this guy being hella sweet, laughing with everyone, and when he introduced himself to me he said: "My name's Mike." I thought he was just another nice guy, and only later did I look back and realize it was Iron Mike Tyson. That night, he was just a sweet kid kickin' it with his homies.

Pretty soon Tyson's arrival was upstaged by Grandmaster Flash, the O.G. Hip Hop god himself. Flash was a pioneer of the Hip Hop game, earning his legendary status with his pioneering DJing skills. Tracy whispered in my ear: "That's Flash!" He'd met him before but it was my first time, and I'd spent years listening to his music. Here I am meeting him! It was so surreal. He was wearing leather pants, fingerless gloves, a double belt, and wore his hair in

DEFINITION OF DOWN

thick-plaited corn rows.

Next knock on the door was Melle Mel. He was already a famous rapper, known for "The Message" and "White Lines." In real life, he was a character, with wild long hair and a deep bass voice. He sported sunglasses and tight fitted jeans. You couldn't help but notice his buff physique under his football jersey. I'm so glad I have a photo of us from that night, where I'm wearing a short black mini skirt and silver lamé blouse that Tracy bought me on that trip.

I felt like a little Hip Hop princess. We piled into cars and gypsy cabs. The illegal cabbies were the only drivers willing to take us to and from the Bronx, and we rolled up to the legendary Palladium nightclub. It was *the* place to be in New York at that time, and the line outside was down the block. This night would mark the beginning of Tracy and me going right to the front of the line. We were mobbed up with the biggest names in rap and the doorman slipped us right behind the velvet rope.

I remember feeling nervous and insecure but trying to play it off for Tracy. Nothing phased him, but I looked around at all these bomb ass people and I felt like a scrub from Riverside, California. Like, how the hell did I get here? I wasn't even 21 yet, barely out of Converse, and I'm looking around at New York club society. The women were dazzling. Some were wearing slinky little dresses and six-inch stilettos with that big '80s hair. Others had bright men's style shirts and shoulder pads with leggings and thigh high boots. There were women in gold bodysuits, baby boll dresses, sequins, lots of sequins. I was taking notes.

I had no makeup on and felt underdressed, but Tracy made me feel like I was the belle of the ball. Before he'd introduce me to people, he'd whisper the pertinent facts in my ear. "Okay, now you're about to meet the founder of Def Jam Records," he'd say. Then I'd be shaking hands with Rick Rubin. Now he's known as a bearded rock god, but at the time I met him, he was so young with just a hint of scruff. He was with photographer Glen E. Friedman that night, and Friedman and I would become great friends over the years. Glen

would play a big part in shaping Tracy's image and ultimately mine. But that night, he was just another cool guy in an amazing scene.

As blown away as I was meeting New York royalty, I found out later they were equally stoked to meet a California girl. Friedman would take my look and expose it all over the world with his incredible photos on the now-famous *Power* album. It's funny that Tracy tried to lure me that first night we met with a line about being on an album cover, but dreams do come true.

As I looked around the Palladium in wonder, I kept thinking, how is it that a young Mexican girl from Corona ended up here? I looked at Tracy with so much pride. As he was making his way through the room, shaking hands like the West Coast Ambassador of Rap, he charmed everyone. I swear, if there'd been babies in there, he woulda picked 'em up and kissed them. You could just see how much love New York was giving him. By making the decision to go to New York to get his deal and ingratiating himself with the O.G.'s of the East Coast, he paved the way for outsiders to come get theirs.

I look back on the night and realize it was our debut as the first couple of rap. Tracy was always by my side. He made it clear to everyone that we were together, unlike a lot of so-called players who hid their women and wives in the background. He told me, "We're doing this. It's just the beginning, but we are doing this."

We went back to the Marriott around 4 a.m. and ordered room service. I remember thinking, man, just a couple months ago we were trying to scrounge up enough coins to split a meal at Chicken Delight. Now, we can actually order two meals. That trip was a turning point because the days of stressing over how we were gonna eat were behind us.

Tracy was born with game, but that trip to New York exposed him to key players who took things to a whole other level. Not just the artists we met, but the record company execs. Seymour Stein was the exec at Warner Bros. that really got what Tracy was about. Stein had signed Madonna and the Ramones, and when he heard Tracy's music, he had the guts to give him a deal with total creative freedom. The fact that Tracy and Islam had already recorded a complete album's worth of material allowed them to get the record out that much faster.

We flew back to L.A. on top of the world, first-class. I'm trippin' off all the room we had, the way the stewardess made sure she took care of us, and Tracy was eating it up. First thing we did when we landed was pick up our girl Felony.

My family sees me roll up in the BMW, Gucci boots and custom-made jewelry, and it was like a homegirl homecoming. Local girl makes good. My grandmother, Connie, comes running out to the driveway and says: "Oooh, everyone's checking you out. Everyone's looking over here, checking the car out. Look at the neighbors peeking through the curtains. Look at Juan across the street pretending to water his lawn."

I was so excited to give my family the gifts I'd brought from New York. No one could believe I'd gotten on a plane and gone to New York City.

When we got back to L.A., our first order of business was to get a new place to live. We'd outgrown our disco love pad and could actually afford a two-bedroom apartment. Tracy also realized we could get another dog, and that's exactly what we did. This time, we didn't have to grab a pup out of a cardboard box on Hollywood Boulevard. We got our first English Bulldog from a breeder who advertised in Pennysaver magazine. Chopper, a little white runt who squinted like Popeye, was the sweetest lil tough guy. For Felony and Chopper, it was love at first sight. They were such awesome buddies.

We found an apartment in the heart of Hollywood, right at the foothills near the Hollywood Bowl. His first major album, *Rhyme Pays*, was just about to drop, and he started giving interviews there.

His designer alter ego, *Antoine*, had reappeared and decked out our place with bright red carpeting, a classic black hand chair with the fingers that cupped you as you sat, and a glass coffee table propped up by a sculpted black panther.

The photo shoot for *Rhyme Pays* consisted of me putting on bikini bottoms with a top I'd cut up super short and fitted. I wore the gun necklace Tracy had made in New York, and we were sitting in the old Porsche, which now had a fresh coat of paint. Glen E. Friedman took the photo and he went for the classic Cali look, even down to the palm trees.

There was so much excitement brewing in the streets of South Central because Warner Bros., through its subsidiary Sire Records, was hyping *Rhyme Pays* on the radio, and local stations started

DEFINITION OF DOWN

playing the single "6 in the Mornin'" before the release of the record. It was a totally different sound from the East Coast because it was a different state of mind. His rhymes broke new ground as they spoke of the gang culture he'd grown up with. Although he was born on the East Coast, he grew up in South Central Los Angeles, an orphan raised by an uncaring aunt. Aside from his homeboys, he was alone in the world, and when he met me, I became his family. It truly was me and him against the world. The fact that his music was about to have a major impact on the world didn't change things between us. We needed each other. He always told me: "It's me and you. 24/7."

The fact that I was a Mexican girl made me long for a kid. Even at 18, in my culture, you're an old maid if you got a man and no kid. He got the dogs to placate me, but I yearned for a child. It would be years before he relented because he had a plan and wanted us to do things the right way. He had a daughter before he met me, and that forced him to go into the Army. He felt bad he couldn't properly support her, and he didn't want for us to start out that way. Tracy was on a mission.

He was the "L.A. Player: MC Ice-T," and he was about to go global.

8 DOPE JAM TOUR

It was all so jazz. People talk about the early days of jazz, when everyone was broke, singing for their supper, playing music till the early hours, going to clubs every night and everyone in the scene knew each other. That's how it was with Hip Hop.

L.A.'s community was tight knit, and Tracy was the leader of the growing rap movement. His hustle would not only pave the way for N.W.A., King T, Too Short and Sir Mix-A-Lot, legitimizing West Coast rap, but it would go on to inspire an entire genre: gangster rap. He always thought of it as just reality, his reality, and he used to call it "reality rap." Before I met him he lived that hardcore street life, and most of his homeboys were still living that life. As he went legit, he tried to take as many people with him as he could. A lot of his homeboys would go on tour with him, he'd find them jobs doing merch, sound, tour managing, or even just handling our bags. He never cut his ties with the streets of South L.A., and even when you watch the early videos, it's always at friend's homes in South Central. He always kept it real, and that's one of the reasons he got so much love and respect.

1987. Here we are watching his album blow up, singles poppin' on KDAY, people recognizing him on the street, and we get a call from the label: "You're going out on tour!"

We'd hit the bigtime! It was the Dope Jam Tour: rap's first big national arena tour to also include a West

DEFINITION OF DOWN

Coast rapper, and Tracy wanted me by his side. The tour was gonna be four months long, and we even got to pick our tour bus. It was the biggest one we could find, and the first thing Tracy did was invite Biz Markie to share our bus. Till this day, whenever I see Biz it's like family.

Imagine this: Public Enemy, Eric B. & Rakim, Doug E. Fresh, Slick Rick, Boogie Down Productions, Kool Moe Dee, Biz Markie and Ice T, all on the same tour. Rap was still so fresh and new, and we had no idea how Tracy would be received outside of L.A. The first night of the tour was in Austin, Texas, and when he hit the stage, the crowd went nuts.

They knew his music! We couldn't believe it. They were singing along to his lyrics. It was surreal because we didn't know how the crowd would feel, but they knew who he was and they showed him so much love. It was like that night after night, each city the artists performed to sold out crowds and I used to pinch myself to make sure it was real. This was really going down. I mean, every night I'm watching Tracy from the side of the stage, and as soon as he was finished, he'd grab my hand and we'd go out into the crowd and watch our favorite artists perform because we were fans! We did this night after night after night. We filmed the entire tour, documenting it because we knew it was so special.

Tracy's set looked elaborate, but since everything on tour comes out of an artist's pocket, he'd put Antoine in charge of design. Antoine conjured up a cop car made out of wood that looked real but was just an excellent replica. It had a siren that would go off and Tracy could jump on top of it and perform. He was smart, though, because other acts spent a lot of money on props; and the way Tracy had it rigged, he actually made money on the tour despite being one of the opening acts. He was determined to make rhyme pay, and he succeeded in doing it.

Living with Biz was a blast. My face hurt from constant laughter, he was so entertaining. Biz was always clowning, and we made a sport out of watching the groupies exit the hotel rooms and tour buses from town to town every morning. No one would ever want to admit who was with who, so Biz and I would try to figure it out.

"Did you see that midget walk out of the hotel just now?" I'd say. "Was she with you Biz, or was she with DJ Evil E?"

Biz would immediately turn it into a song, but no one would ever cop to who they slept with the night before. We called it the Walk of Shame. Groupies were everywhere, and one time, Biz was rolling backstage on a bicycle and he pulled a girl's ponytail. It came off in his hand, and he was holding it up like a flag.

Backstage, male groupies would hit on me. Some took it too far, and when I couldn't shake this one guy, Professor Griff and Public Enemy's S1Ws came to my rescue. It was just like that. We were a big family, the East Coast and the West Coast coming together. When we weren't at arenas, we were poolside in cheap hotels or trying to find the nearest mall.

We had paper. The guys would buy sneakers, and I'd get new bikinis. Money was burning a hole in our pocket, and we'd just look for some bullshit to spend it on.

Tracy was smart because he kept his merch rights. So many artists would sell their merchandise rights for a big chunk of change, but then that was it. They didn't own their property any more. Tracy, on the other hand, did it right. He had an excellent attorney, financial manager and accountant and they advised him well.

Antoine designed the shirts and they sold big. The hot seller was a white crew neck with a big "T" in the center with the word "Ice" graffiti'd and an Uzi in the middle of the "T." He definitely knew his image, and he controlled it all the way. In Kansas City, some of Tracy's boys gave a bootlegger a beat down because he was selling Ice T shirts that weren't Ice T sanctioned. That was a big no-no, and they took his wad away.

We became friends with KRS-One, who's one of the nicest guys on earth. People were so intimidated by him because he's so smart, but he's also really humble. We watched his set every night for four months, riveted to each word. Flavor Flav and Chuck D were at the height of their fame and people would do anything just to be near them. Flava was cut from the same cloth as Biz and the two of them were a circus sideshow unto themselves. Chuck was quiet and laid back, soaking it all in, and he really embraced Tracy and me. He respected Tracy's music and where he was coming from, and the respect was definitely mutual.

It had been less than a year since I'd quit my job. I was still a kid and I was living this crazy wonderful life, going from town to town with artists who I would have bought tickets to see. I would have been first in line for the Dope Jam Tour. But I was Tracy's girl and I was backstage, I was on the bus, I was in the videos, and I was about to become famous.

9 POWER

It's been a quarter century since the Dope Jam Tour, and it was a turning point for rap. When we started the tour, people were still mumbling about rap being a fad that wouldn't last. When we finished the tour, it was clear there was money to be made in this game. In some ways, it was the beginning of the end. Those days were the best because it was all so fresh, and it had a real innocence to it.

But truly, it was a business and Tracy got down to business. By traveling the country and hearing the response from fans, he realized he was getting through to people. Even more importantly, he realized he had power.

After we got back from tour, *Rhyme Pays* was at the top of the rap charts, and we were flush with enough cash to pay off our apartment a year in advance. Having money in the bank for the first time felt really good, but we also had to change a few things. People were starting to recognize us wherever we'd go, and we got tons of love from people. But Tracy was mindful of the fact that you also become a mark for haters, people who want what you have.

He'd always tell me, "I don't want you to have to change, but just be aware of your surroundings." He knew I preferred swap meets to high-end retail any day, but we were now having to be smart. Tracy understood and tolerated the haters; he had a way of either ignoring them or confronting them in a style where he could just shut it down. Mostly, it was simply because he was smarter than everyone else and knew how to outwit them.

One night in Westwood, we were leaving a movie premiere and a Latino guy in the crowd started heckling us. He kept referring to me being Latina. Even though this was the late '80s, it was still a hot issue that we were an interracial couple. This dude kept on after Tracy, saying: "You can't even get a sister. You have to come after our women." Tracy kept smiling, waving to the crowd of fans. Meanwhile, I'm freaking out, nudging him: "Do you hear what that guy's saying?" Tracy, without even changing the grin on his face, says through his teeth: "Yeah, I hear him. So what? He wants attention and ignoring him is the best way to shut him down. Let's roll, babe." He never let it faze him. It totally turned me on that he handled it the way he did. He was teaching me so much, and one thing was to never let busters rile you up. His friend, however, wasn't taking it so well and went and chased the guy to give him a beat down. He chased him all through the streets of UCLA with the guy yelling, "Help me! Help me!" Even the guy's friends stepped aside and let Tracy's pal have at him. Tracy just laughed at the whole thing, how this dude was a tough guy one minute and a total sucker the next, running like a coward.

I was not only in love with him because he was loving and caring, but he was such a badass. I'd listen to his interviews, and he was not only schooling the listeners, he was schooling me. He was so articulate and so approachable for his fans, and there was nobody like him.

You could never predict what he was gonna say about anything. Just when you thought you'd have his rap down, he'd flip the script and say something totally unpredictable. He was a street intellectual and some of the things he'd say just blew my mind.

At this point, people were starting to see what a rare person he truly was and how deep he was. Even the way he treated me publicly was unique. He put me front and center with everything he did. He talked about me in interviews, he called me his queen in liner notes and he started including me in his work more and more. I was not only being recognized as the cover girl for *Rhyme Pays,* but all the music magazines and urban magazines began to include photos of us every month.

I started getting requests to model and to host talk shows. I was starring in Tracy's music videos, and day by day, it became clear we were rap's first power couple. Most of the rappers even today keep their women behind the scenes, waaaay behind the scenes. Tracy was proud of me and of us, and he wanted the world to know about it.

While we were on the Dope Jam Tour, he'd been writing lyrics on the bus, in hotels, on planes, whenever he could get a break, getting ready for his next album. His interviews were being noticed by people in Hollywood. He was tapped to write the theme song to a movie that would become a major game changer, *Colors,* a film that exposed L.A.'s gang wars. Not only did Hollywood execs tap him to create the song, but they turned to him for advice on just how real this war was in L.A. He'd been rapping about it for years by then, but it took the shooting death of an Asian woman in Westwood for people to start to wake up. The *Colors* theme song really defined that era, and here again, it took us to a whole other level. He wasn't someone just known in the rap game, but he'd made the transition to writing the theme song for a blockbuster movie. The fact that his music helped fuel the success showed just how mainstream rap was becoming. The video for "Colors" still holds up a quarter century later. As much as he respected the bangers out there doing what they got to do to survive, he continued to caution kids to try to avoid that lifestyle.

The success of "Colors" helped prime the pump for *Power.* People were excited to hear what he had to say next, and he didn't disappoint his fans.

He was laid back about pretty much everything, but I remember when he told me about the photo shoot for *Power.* He said, "Get ready. We're gonna do this next album cover. Do what you gotta do to get yourself where you wanna be because this is gonna be a

DEFINITION OF DOWN

big deal." So I went and tightened up my perm and got a little sun. I didn't know what I was going to wear. I'd worn a mismatched bikini on the first album, and I thought this time I'd bring a few risqué options. I went down to Hollywood Blvd. and bought five bathing suits. One in each color. The day came when it was time to do the shoot, and our friend Glen E. Friedman told us to meet him at a photo studio. Tracy told me to pack whatever I wanted, and I loaded up all the options I had. Along with the bathing suits, I brought some slinky little dresses.

I didn't even know what he had planned until I saw the guns. He said, "We're all going to hold guns, and the only one you'll see from the front will be D's." I'm thinking, cool. I'd gotten my first gun at 11 years old, and I thought it would be a powerful statement to see a woman holding a gun.

He handed me a sawed-off shotgun, also known as a riot pump.

I started unpacking the clothes I'd brought, and he grabbed that white, one-piece bathing suit right out of the suitcase. I remember walking out of the dressing room and he said, "Yep. That's the one." He also chose my red high heel pumps and matching earrings. He handpicked everything.

It was Antoine in full effect. Not only did he have that interior decorator streak, but he was so into fashion. And that included my fashion. He wanted the shoes and the earrings to be matchy-matchy, and when I looked in the mirror, I had to admit I looked bomb. I had so much self-confidence and a lot of that was driven by his approval, because he was incredibly complimentary all the time.

I did my own hair and makeup, believe it or not. It wasn't Glen's style to shoot a staged photo with a woman. He was known for capturing skaters, punks and rappers in their element. But this was gonna be different. Tracy was making a statement with this photo spread, and we were all along for the ride.

When I strutted onto the set, Glen blushed a little bit and then it was on to business. He'd tell me to move my shoulders back, put my chin up, stand up straight, which wasn't easy because that sawed off shotgun was frickin' heavy and I was wearing heels.

Tracy was standing right behind Glen, and he added his own instructions. I can remember it like it was yesterday. I was a little nervous, but Tracy made me feel so good and secure. It was like that with him all the time. I never knew where the day was going to take us and I just didn't care because he made me feel so safe.

I spent about two hours posing in that suit, and then me and DJ Evil E took turns wearing our one gold bracelet, cheating to make it look like we each had one. I also wore the infamous gun pendant that Tracy had made in the village on our first trip to New York. Tracy and DJ Evil E shared Tracy's Rolex watch during the shoot, making it look like Evil had it going on as well. After I'd exhausted every pose in the white suit, we then shot the photo for the single "I'm Your Pusher" and for that I put on the red bathing suit. That photo is also scandalous, because it shows a real closeup of my curves from the side with a big close-up of Tracy's smirking face.

In that photo, you can see a ring Tracy had given me as a commitment to our relationship. He felt that putting me front and center with that ring on his album covers said everything about how he felt about me. I look back and think, there really was no one like him. Even till this day, I realize there is no one like Tracy Marrow.

When I look at the *Power* album today, I also realize there's really no one out there like me. I mean, for its time, it was so racy. But I look at that cover photo, and I am so proud of it because it says "power", just the photo alone. It may have something to do with that mad dog look on my face, a little mean mugging, but that's real. That's a real part of who I am and where I'm from.

It wasn't until a few days after the shoot when I realized just how explosive the album cover could get. We went to Warner Bros. to look at the proofs and everyone at the label was so excited about it. They really trusted Tracy and they had his back. I saw the photos and thought, Oh, shit, we did it now! I knew it was going to get

DEFINITION OF DOWN

some attention, and I immediately thought of my family. I'd already done *Rhyme Pays,* but I wasn't holding a gun and I wasn't exposing as much of my backside. I decided then and there that the moment I had a copy of the record in my hand I was going to have to pay a visit to Grandma's house.

* * * * * *

Let me take you on a little trip down memory lane to this thing called a record store. It was a place filled with vinyl, and people hung out there night and day to get hot new releases. They'd line up at midnight for a new release, and it was a way of life for a lot of folks. Warner Bros. booked us on a whirlwind tour to promote the record, so we made stops in record stores and radio stations throughout the country and internationally. Fans were lining up to get our autographs, and the record was literally sailing off the shelves.

Power was a hit.

Nowadays, everyone seems overexposed and nothing's shocking, but that record in 1988 was a big deal. It was embraced by the rap community immediately. They loved his hardcore sound and the iconic imagery. I had become the Farrah Fawcett cover girl for the Hip Hop world. Felt like everyone had that poster in their rooms and that album on their turntable. Tracy didn't suffer any sophomore slump. He was two for two. The radio hosts always high-fived me, giving me my props.

Even Glen was blown away by the success. In his book *Fuck You Heroes,* he says he had no idea how huge that picture would become.

Needless to say, with any success you can also plan on haters to crawl out of the woodwork. It took awhile for the controversy to start. Initially, the response to the record was overwhelmingly positive, but then a series of articles started popping up by feminists who condemned my pictures as being degrading to women. They also tried to play me as a victim.

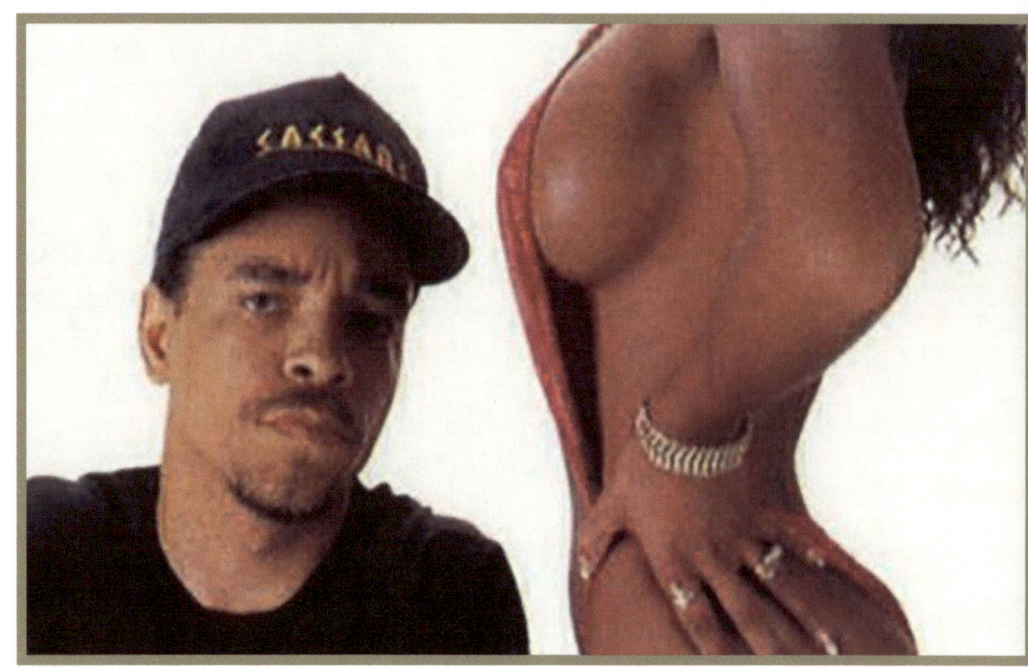

In addition, the fact that the *Power* album also contained Tracy's idea of a love song, "Let's Get Butt Naked and Fuck," sparked more controversy. The feminist writers weren't feeling that one either.

I thought the song was funny as all hell.

True to my word, I took the album to Grandma's house. When she saw the photo, she said: "Mija, you look so pretty and strong, such a strong Mexican girl. I don't care for the way your suit goes up your butt but, mija, you look so beautiful."

I figured, if Grandma was cool with it, then I was good. She also knew that Tracy and I were together, and he was showing me off to the world. He was proud to be with me, and I was proud to be with him.

That cover sealed the deal. We were now officially the King and Queen of Rap. People on the street would call me "Darlene the Queen," because that's what he called me. I was nobody's victim. I was a girl in love, and I was proud of my man.

DEFINITION OF DOWN

As more and more feminist groups condemned the *Power* album cover and even indicated his lyrics could promote rape, there came a time for us to defend our art. And where better to do this than on *Oprah*. Back in the late '80s, Oprah was blowing the hell up and so was the PMRC, the Parental Music Resource Center. Man, we've come a long way since those days when Tipper Gore and her political allies determined that music needed a stamp on the cover indicating whether or not content was appropriate for children. They were known as the Washington wives and their stated goal was to increase parental control over music deemed to have violence, drug reference or sexual content. Sounds simple enough, but it elicited a shitstorm, and Tracy was at the wheel driving the bus. Frank Zappa was riding shotgun.

Tracy felt the wave of censorship coming his way and hurting other artists who were also pushing the envelope with their work, which is why he titled his next album, *Freedom of Speech... Just Watch What You Say*. Increasingly, he believed the government was circling the wagons, and he felt the PMRC was just the tip of the iceberg.

I used to lie awake truly frightened for him, because he really had no one to help him fight his battles. I was there staunchly by his side, but I could see there was no manager or agent who could really step up and take the lead. Tracy had to wage his own wars. To the public, he always put on a brave face. In private, I could see the fight taking its toll. His record label still backed him up, but no one could predict just how fierce this fight would get.

The day before we were scheduled to be on *Oprah*, we were flown to Chicago and put up at a swanky four-star hotel. I could see the view of Lake Michigan and the famed Chicago Loop. Tracy was going to be a featured guest, sitting right next to Tipper Gore, the then-wife of future vice president Al Gore.

Tracy was excited about being on Oprah's show, and we got up early to make sure we were the first ones on the set. Oprah also arrived early, and she came out with no shoes and just kicked it with us on the set before the show. She was so sweet and she told us how everything was gonna go down. When the show taped I was in the audience, and I could hear snickering coming from the women in the row in front of me. Turns out, Tipper had stacked the deck with PMRC members strewn throughout the live audience. Tracy could see things getting heated between me and some of the women in the crowd, and he pointed to me and introduced me as his wife and suggested they ask me directly if I take this stuff seriously.

Oprah worked her way over to me, and there's a classic clip that's still all over YouTube of me defending the word "bitch" and his right to inject humor and satire in his lyrics.

I wasn't expecting to be interviewed but I shot right up and said, "When he calls a bitch a bitch... you don't see me turn around." I could see him beaming with pride, his dimples and smile lighting up my way. We always had each other's back, even on the glaring national spotlight of *Oprah*.

The articles written about us during this time really say it all.

If there's one thing we really needed, it was a vacation. We'd been working since the day we met and Tracy had "aloha" on his mind. The last time he was in Hawaii, he was stationed there in the Army. He hadn't taken a legit trip back, and he was so excited because we had money, and he told me to book us a vacation. I didn't waste any time.

We went to Maui first, and it was dreamy. The room faced the ocean, and we were so excited to be there. We did all the tourist things. We went to a luau and we got a convertible car and drove all over the island. At one romantic dinner, we ran into Herbie Hancock. Tracy was in awe, because Herbie lived on the island and had a studio there.

It was a lover's paradise, and we soaked up every minute.

Next stop was Oahu, where he'd been stationed as a young Army grunt. He couldn't wait to show me his base. Even though he was living an honest life by then, he still felt sketchy about going too

DEFINITION OF DOWN

near the base, like he'd done something wrong and might get caught.

He took me to the North Shore and showed me the hardcore surfers out there. It started raining on us as we were driving around in a convertible, and he didn't care. He never cared about things like that, and I always appreciated it. He was so dang chill.

We'd been together for a few years by then, but I was still learning what I can and can't say to him. Even though he was very chill, he still had certain idiosyncrasies. And as a man, there were things he didn't want to be challenged on.

Apparently, his scuba diving technique was one of them. We'd decided to take diving lessons to get certified, and we both had the same instructor and we received the same information.

We went to take our first dive, and this fool was so excited. We were videotaping everything by then, and as we went further down, I noticed that Tracy wasn't releasing the pressure from his mask, and I also noticed he wasn't following all the instructions.

He was doing that whole ghetto schlep, like he was gonna do it his way. I swam up to him, concerned about the mask's pressure, and I gestured toward the mask, and he just put his hand up and waved me off like, "I know what I'm doing."

I'm thinking to myself, I'm gonna listen to what the white man is saying. I'm gonna follow protocol. I'm not doing no barrio schlep. I'm following instructions. Damn straight.

And guess who came out unscathed from her first dive? Me.

Didn't work out so well for Tracy though.

As he came up from his dive and took his mask off, I heard a collective gasp from everyone on the boat.

I looked over at him and omigawd! It was the creature from the black lagoon. His eyes were popped out of his eye sockets, and it was the scariest looking thing. He looked like a black Marty Feldman.

The instructor said: "Damn it! You didn't release the pressure!"

I was just sitting there, biting my tongue, thinking to myself, Um huh.

Tracy was trying to shrug it off but then caught a glimpse of himself in a mirror. "Oh, shit!" he said. He couldn't play this one off.

The instructor wouldn't let him dive anymore. He had to sit out the next two dives. Meanwhile, I got certified.

His scary eyes looked like that all night, and finally, the next morning it was gone. Thank God.

This trip was pivotal for so many reasons, but one thing I recall is just how close I felt to him and how much he poured his love out for me. And it was moments like that that gave me the courage to talk to him about marriage and our future. Holy matrimony was not his favorite subject and it took courage to even bring it up. It was always on my mind.

He started shooting me the same old bullshit, but every time he did, he'd always have a new angle on it. It always got deeper. I was so young that it was easy to get me all twisted up.

Here's what he said in Hawaii: "Darlene, if it's a ring you want, and that'll make you feel safer or more secure, then I'll get you a bunch of rings. But I don't believe in marriage. It's too traditional for us. What we have is deeper than most people who just went for the paperwork. Look at Goldie Hawn and Kurt Russell. They're happy. Most rappers, you don't even know about their girl, they keep them hidden in the background. But look at us, everyone knows we're together."

I'd see his lips move and think to myself, Oh, here we go again...

wa wa wa... It would be the sound of the teacher from *Peanuts*.

I'd nod my head and say, "Right... right... right, no you're right... I feel you..." But that was mostly a lie.

Eventually, I would get an opening and shoot back, "But it's what I want. You know I'm not gonna do you wrong. You should know that. Plus, I'm Mexican. We go for the traditional stuff like marriage and kids."

He'd say, "Watch, we're gonna be together a lot longer than most couples."

He kept referring to marriage as "The Papers," reducing it all down to paperwork.

Even though I'd accept his words, it killed me inside. I wanted to be his wife. And you can imagine my family asking me questions about it.

In all his interviews, he'd refer to me as his wife, even sending me love letters addressed to "Darlene Marrow," but when it came to making it official, he thought he knew best. I look back now and realize he did know best. He knew what was best for him.

I had to try to get over it, but it wasn't easy. Especially on that beautiful island where romance was everywhere.

He did buy me rings though, and after that trip, he bought me one in particular to surprise me with, a gold and solitaire diamond ring. It was beautiful, and I was grateful. But I so wanted to be married to him, for real.

* * * * * *

Despite the lack of paperwork, there was no doubt we were rap's reigning power couple, and as we achieved more fame and infamy and his signature soundtrack style was being heard in films, his movie star cache was on the rise. He began getting more film offers. And these were a nice step up from *Breakin'*.

His first big opportunity came from the bathroom at Power Tools, the hottest nightclub in L.A. during the late '80s. As the legend goes, Mario Van Peebles heard Tracy's voice in the stall next to his and said: "I've been trying to find you! You're my Scotty Appleton."

Tracy and Mario were in that bathroom forever, setting up the *New Jack City* deal. It was on.

Tracy came out of the bathroom with Mario and they were both beaming because they knew they were gonna kick some ass, even though Tracy was trippin' because he was gonna play a cop. Mario told him he was perfect and said, "Dude! You're acting. If you can play a cop, the total opposite of you, you can play anything."

Tracy looked at me when he finally got out of the bathroom and said, "Baby, pack your bags."

We were going to New York.

MAKIN' MOVIES & A BABY

In 1990, a black film cast was a big deal. When we got the list of the actors who'd been cast, we were so excited because nothing had really been done like this before. Not only was Mario directing a screenplay written by a black screenwriter, but the cast included Wesley Snipes, Chris Rock, Allen Payne, Vanessa A. Williams, Tracy Camilla Johns, Michael Michele, Bill Nunn, Bill Cobbs, Christopher Williams and such music artists as Flavor Flav, Teddy Riley, Guy, Keith Sweat, the O'Jays and the Levert Brothers.

People say movie sets are boring, but this one was so exciting. We knew it was going to be groundbreaking and so did the fans on the streets of New York where we were filming. People gave us big ups everywhere we went. Tracy and Chris Rock bonded on the set and in between takes, they'd be choppin' it up with the New York fans.

Till this day, I don't know why no one stopped me, but I had a handheld camera and was filming during the entire shoot. Tracy told them I'd be filming and no one stopped me. Even when there were closed sets, I just kept rolling the film.

Every night after he filmed, we'd go back to the small apartment we were sharing and get busy. The excitement of everything made it easy to be in an amorous mood.

Just being in that big beautiful city was exciting. I'm so glad I got to experience it when it was still gritty

DEFINITION OF DOWN

New York. Even though Tracy was working hard, we had so much fun each day. Everyone was so cool, and the energy was electric because the people involved knew they had a hit on their hand. The film was based on the crack wars of the '80s, and the soundtrack went on to be a monster success.

It was pretty damn great. This was the big time. His salary was getting bigger and we really started rolling. It meant so much to me that I was able to help my family. I was finally in a position to support them the way I'd always wanted to, and Tracy was incredibly generous. I was able to buy my grandparents new recliners, a new TV, new couches. If anyone needed anything, we were there to help out. Even ol' Rose.

Rose called out of the blue, and I asked her how she was doing. She told me her car was broken, and I got off the phone and told Tracy. "Ol' Rosie's claiming broke," I told him. "That's fine," he said. "You know in your heart of hearts you want to help her out." He was just cool like that.

I'll never forget what it felt like. The level we were at was amplified, and we were able to do a lot for not only ourselves and everyone else, but we could do it without a care in the world. That was the best, and that's what I miss the most. Being able to do all those extras for people.

People were always pressuring me, telling me, "Now, you should start treating yourself to better things. You should go to a fancy, high-end hair stylist." I was still doing those things all by myself. But friends pushed me and said, "You should get a taste of the high end."

So like a sucka I went to Bumble and Bumble in New York. I hated the whole experience, going through three to four people to get my hair done. Spending all that money made my feel sick to my stomach. It just wasn't me.

We did go on some pretty major shopping sprees. We went to the

Village boutiques and to Saks Fifth Avenue. We wouldn't even necessarily buy anything, but just the fact that we could go in these high-end shops, and if we saw something we liked we could buy it. That's what was cool.

But we were also stacking our chips, because we were getting close to that home buying time. Antoine was intent on bigger and better when it came to home living, so we did need to save our dough. Still, with movie stardom everything kicked up.

We flew everywhere first class, we were treated better wherever we went. Restaurants always seemed to have a good table for us. The quality of the restaurants got better. I was still D from Corona, so more money for me meant more money to go to the swap meet.

The party invites kept coming. We started hanging out with big movie stars, with known people, and I cheesed my way from L.A. to New York.

One of the biggest parties we attended during the *New Jack* time was Flavor Flav's birthday bash. Public Enemy was big-time in New York and Afrika Bambaataa was there, all the hot people that were happening at that time. It was kinda like the *New Jack Swingers* set. We'd go to Teddy Riley's parties. Keith Sweat. I loved being around these people because we listened to their music, and you gotta respect the feeling. The industry parties were getting bigger and better. The biggest party was the Soul Train Awards. The parties were so lavish. I loved the MTV Awards, the Grammy Awards.

I remember being at one of Clive Davis' pre-parties with Aretha Franklin and Quincy Jones, and here we are fraternizing with these people. That was the year Tracy won a Grammy for Quincy's *Back on the Block* album. Aretha Franklin was sitting at our table, and Tracy leaned over and said, "Can my girl take a photo with you?" Of course, she was so frickin' sweet. She took a photo with me and said, "Baby, come here..." I bent down and cheesed away. Frankie Valli was at our same table, and I remember sneaking outside to call my dad, Pete. "You're never gonna believe who I'm sitting with!" And telling him all about Frankie Valli, and Aretha, Tevin

DEFINITION OF DOWN

Campbell, and Quincy Jones and his daughters.

It was at Flavor Flav's party where we also got a taste of drama. It was the first time where Tracy and LL Cool J ran into each other after LL made his comments about the *Power* album in a song titled "To da Break of Dawn." LL graphically in his own lyrics described how he jerked off to my image, and he busted Tracy's chops for using my image to sell records. It stirred up some early East Coast-West Coast rivalry. Word was getting around at the party that shit was getting ready to go down, but Afrika Bambaataa stopped anything from jumping off. They had a summit right then and there, and they sat at a round table and discussed whatever needed to be done and they worked it out. That's how things were handled back in the day.

LL and Tracy till this day have never been chummy-chummy. Everybody used to tease me, "What if you ever get with LL? That would be the ultimate getback."

Not my style. There would never be any love lost between those two. I remember being at World on Wheels on Venice Blvd. in Mid-City L.A. when LL got mobbed out of there because he was wearing a red Kangol fuzzy hat in Crips territory and he didn't know. He's from New York. He was about to perform, and when he showed up everybody started a ruckus. They knocked over the metal detectors.

It was nuts! He made it through a song or two before things got too heated. But they ran him and his crew the hell out of there.

Those days were all so crazy and fun.

* * * * * *

The one downside to being a movie star was the impact it had on Tracy's hair. For *New Jack City*, he had to wear dreadlocks, and no matter how hard we tried, we couldn't get those damn dreads out of his hair. We had to buy all these products from a beauty supply store, and the producers wanted him to keep the extensions in, just in case he needed to do some pick-up shots. But this fool was done. They'd fused real dreads into his hair. I remember sitting there for hours, and he's literally falling asleep while I'm doing my best to take the extensions out of his hair. Thanks to that experience, I know a lot about hair now. I'd have to massage the hair grease into his scalp and then get it off his scalp. *New Jack City* was awesome for his career, but lousy for his suave coif.

* * * * * *

After this crazy whirlwind tour of filming, award shows, performances and parties, came the moment every Mexican girl waits for. I was pregnant! I think the success of that film played a big role because both of us felt more secure. You have to remember, it wasn't that long ago that we struggled to put two quarters together, but after making that film, we knew this was real. This career was for real. He'd knocked me up at that sweet little apartment in New York.

When we returned to Los Angeles, we moved to our first proper Hollywood home, a home once owned by Humphrey Bogart and Lauren Bacall. It was in the lower Hollywood Hills, and it was the last home on a block that had been divided into condos and apartments. Axl Rose was our neighbor, and Spago's was right down below. The landscaping was tropical and lush; it was like a Tahitian oasis in the middle of the city. The view was insane. We could see for miles. And I'll never forget when Tracy first saw it. He got that Antoine look on his face, and I could see those wheels spinning in his head.

I knew that place was going to have his distinct style: ghetto moderne. Sure enough, the black leather couches, black hand chair and the black panther table filled out the living room. He added a drop-down movie screen and a mirrored ceiling in our bedroom. And of course, where I'd hoped the swing set would go, he built a 12-seater jacuzzi, which took up what little yard space we had. Oh, Antoine. He was happy, and when he was happy, I was happy. Although I got to say, when my relatives came over, I had a tough time explaining that mirror.

When my grandma saw it, she said: "Oh, mija, that makes the room look so big!" Bless her clueless heart.

I was officially showing a baby bump by the time the premiere for *New Jack City* rolled around. Even though I had wanted a baby for so long, to be honest, I hated being pregnant. Not the fact that I was going to have this baby, I loved that. But I got big as shit! I gained pounds.

Bless Tracy's heart, he still would tell me I looked beautiful. He'd take me on tour with him, and there I was in my high heels and cankles, looking like I was about to explode. My legs were swollen as shit, and they were cylinders, one size all the way down to my toes. Tracy would say to his friends, "Ooh, look at my baby girl. She's fillin' things out. Ain't she hot?!"

I got up to a size 16, but he'd tell me every day how beautiful I looked. All I could do was accessorize. I'd change my eye color with contacts, I'd tighten up my perm, get a little tan, whatever I could do to try to not feel like Jabba the Hutt. I was trying big time, but I look back at those pictures and think, That ain't cute. No matter how he tried to reassure me, I knew I looked fucked up.

Tracy and I always did everything together, and when I got pregnant, he didn't want that to change. But the life of a tour wife wasn't easy when you're waddling around as a 200-pounder flounder.

On Tracy's next film, *Ricochet*, Denzel Washington felt so bad for me he actually had the director put me in the movie. I have a scene where I'm playing a college student, and I was so fat they had to cut the back of my costume and hold it together with pins, because even wardrobe's largest sizes wouldn't fit me.

Here I was, 200 pounds, and Tracy still wanted me to go on tour with Body Count. I was seven months pregnant and I went on tour. I'd go for a week at a time, then I'd fly home and recover. It was an exciting time because Body Count, which was Tracy's speed metal side project, was really starting to resonate with people. He had touched a nerve and his music was exploding. It was an awesome thing to see and he felt so validated that he could switch musical genres and still have an audience. He loved Slayer and Megadeth, and Body Count was his way to pay tribute to that scene while still lyrically staying true to who he was.

Tracy was supposed to be on tour with Body Count the day our son was born. He got a pager that allowed him to be reached globally, and when I called him with the news that we were going to have to induce our baby, he canceled shows so he could be by my side at our son's birth.

I picked him up from the airport, and he'd instructed me to wear a dress without panties, like he always did. Didn't matter that I was big'uns, he thought I looked beautiful and we raced home to make love.

Needless to say, I went into labor that night. Turns out, Tracy was all it took to induce me, and he knew that baby was coming even before I did. I called his name when I thought it was time, and he was already out in front of the house in our Range Rover, honking.

He was ready to go!

DEFINITION OF DOWN

I hoisted myself into the car and didn't realize he'd put the seat all the way back for me like a bed and I nearly fell over. He thought he was helping but I was flailing around like a beached whale. He raced down the hill and in all the excitement he forgot how to get to Cedars-Sinai, the hospital. He got all turned and twisted around and a 15-minute car ride turned into 30. And of course, I can't see out the window, because I'm flat on my back.

We finally got there, and the doctors evaluated me and said I wasn't dilated enough so they wanted me to walk in circles. I spent hours walking the halls with a couple of other ladies, while Tracy holed up on a couch with three other dads who were also waiting in anticipation.

The doctors were just about to send me home, when all of a sudden, woosh! There went the amniotic fluid, all over Tracy's Air Jordans.

They found me a swanky private room and prepared me for the epidural. As soon as he saw the doctor whip out that long-ass needle, he took a hike. He'd been on the phone giving a friend a blow-by-blow of the events, but he couldn't deal with the fact that needle was going into my spine.

Eighteen hours later, as family came and went, Tracy was there by my side helping my breathe and push. He even went to find me a towel to put on my forehead to cool me down.

The nurse told Tracy to come take a look as the baby was beginning to show and he said, "Nah, I'll pass."

She said, "No, seriously, you're gonna wanna see this. This kid has a lot of hair!"

So Tracy went to look, and I heard him say, "Wooooah! This lil fool does have a lot of hair!"

The baby boy arrived at 11:17 pm on November 21, 1991, during Thanksgiving week. And we did have much to be thankful for. He

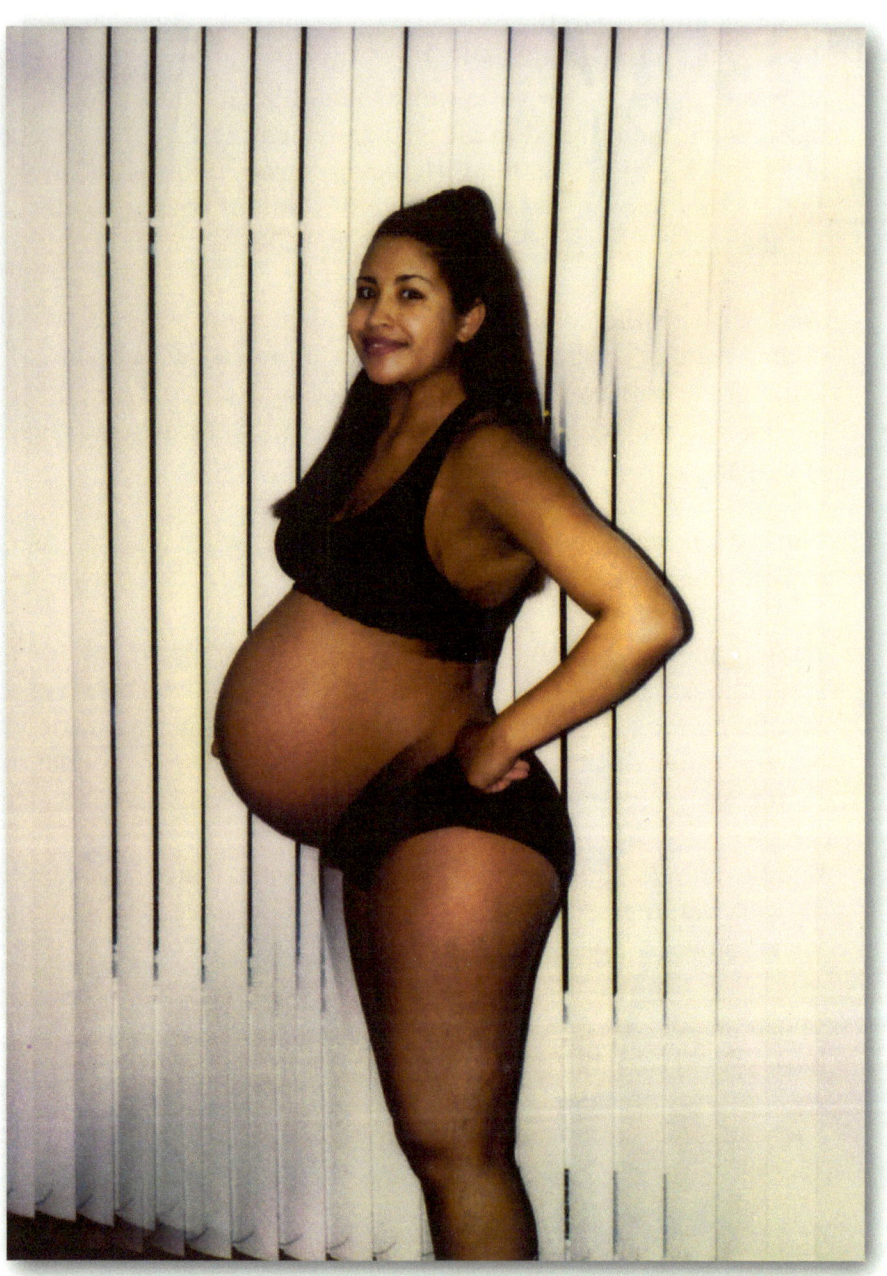

was a healthy 9 pounds, had all his fingers and toes, and the nurse was right, he had gobs of hair.

Tracy was cheesing, documenting the entire process with photos. I was not only proud of our son, I was proud of his father's involvement that night. When it came time for the doctor to sew me up, after he'd given me an episiotomy, he asked me if I'd like a few extra stitches. Before I could answer, Tracy said, "Sure!" Everyone had a good laugh.

That beautiful, long-haired, nekked boy felt good in my arms. He was smiling the moment he was born and he looked so much like my father, Pete. I also saw Tracy's dimples and knew he'd be a ladies' man. He was so beautiful. I had in my mind that we were going to name him Solomon, after Tracy's father. I couldn't wait to call him Sonny for short. But Tracy had other ideas.

The next day at the hospital when the nurse was taking down his name, Tracy said: "We're going to name him ICE."

And she said, "Ike?"

And he said, "No. ICE. I-C-E. All capital letters. It's not a name, it's a statement."

I looked at the nurse, and she commiserated with me.

He turned around to me and said, "You know, baby, everyone's gonna call him Lil Ice. It's just gonna happen. So let's make it official." The truth is, he was right. We could've named him Mark or Jesus, and everyone would still call him Lil Ice.

So, in all caps, ICE Tracy Marrow received his name.

Looking back on those days, it brings back such sweet memories. It was our greatest joy, but our son's birth would also change the dynamic of our relationship forever.

I

THERE GOES THE NEIGHBORHOOD

Needless to say, Tracy wanted a bigger crib. I loved our Bogie and Bacall love shack, but he had bigger ambitions. He always had bigger ambitions.

The hunt was on for a larger house. But first, he had a Body Count tour to finish. He'd just finished the first Lollapalooza, which introduced his music to an entirely new audience. Once again, he'd climbed another level.

He was becoming an international superstar, and superstars don't get there without sacrifice. Part of that sacrifice included us. Despite the glow of new motherhood, I quickly discovered I was basically a single parent. The day-to-day caring of our son was up to me, and I was still a young woman. It was pretty intimidating.

He had to go back on the road three days after Lil Ice was born, and we were essentially on our own. My big Mexican family shared in the joy of his birth, but they lived 90 miles away. They did come pick me up for Thanksgiving, because I was too afraid to drive with my little newborn.

On top of that, I was getting calls from our realtor who was scoping out new possibilities for us. I wasn't about to step on Antoine's toes. That was his department. But I gave him the messages and he already had his eye on a sweet Sunset Plaza house, high up in the hills above the Sunset Strip.

Despite his constant work schedule, he tried to be a good father, regularly checking in and calling from wherever

DEFINITION OF DOWN

he was. He would always make it to our son's school functions when he was in town. He took us traveling and boating; the three of us did everything together that we possibly could.

But he wasn't truly prepared for all that fatherhood entailed. It was clear he had issues over the amount of time being a mother took away from our relationship. In some ways, he was jealous of his own son. He tried to overcome those feelings, as evidenced in a letter he sent me.

He was used to having things his own way and that included having me when and where he wanted me. I still wanted to be all that for him, but I also had obligations to my son. I was determined to be the best mother ever, and that became my goal in life. I loved Tracy, but I loved this kid too. And there's no doubt, he loved us as well. He was hellbent on taking us on tour with him as much as possible, because he knew at some point, Lil Ice would be in school and that wouldn't work out anymore.

Despite his attempts at normalcy, I could feel something had shifted. Something was off. We were the two closest people ever for years, and I could sense a change.

It was definitely a transitional period for us, and we pushed through it. Once we realized what was happening, we devised all kinds of ways to address the distance. Date nights, touring as a family, my relatives taking Lil Ice for weekends. He also insisted on a housekeeper to help give me a break, even though I didn't want a housekeeper because I loved looking after our home. Nevertheless, we did what we needed to do to keep the flame alive in our relationship while still raising a family.

A few months after the birth of Ice, we took off for Mexico. My family volunteered to take care of the baby for a week and we flew to Acapulco. I'd never been there before, and it was really beautiful. We stayed at the Las Brisas Hotel where each bungalow came with its own Jeep, its own private pool and private garden. He noticed right away there were no phones or a TV, so we spent the nights just

F A S S B I N D   H O T E L S

Neues Kongresshotel

Alle Zimmer unserer Hotels bieten Farbfernsehen mit Gratis-Videofilmen, Radio, Direktwahl-Telefon, Mini-Bar, Telefax und Computeranschluss. Nichtraucherzimmer.

BERN

HOTEL AMBASSADOR**
Seftigenstrasse 99
Tel. (031) 454 111
ab 23.09.93: 031/371 41 11
Fax (031) 454 117
ab 23.09.93: 031/371 41 17
Telex 911 826
Ruhige Lage.
Wunderschöne Aussicht auf das Bundeshaus.
Gratis-Parkplätze, Restaurant, Bar, Hallenschwimmbad.

LAUSANNE

HOTEL AGORA**
Tél. (021) 617 12 11

HOTEL ALPHA**
Tél. (021) 230 131
ab 14.09.93: 021/323 01 31

NEUES HOTEL CITY*
Tél. (021) 202 141
ab 14.09.93: 021/320 21 41

GENF

HOTEL CRISTAL**
Tél. (022) 731 34 00

LUGANO

HOTEL CONTINENTAL*
Tél. (091) 561 212

Kongresszentrum FH:
Bern   Hotel Ambassador
Lausanne Hotel Agora
          Hotel Alpha

DEAR DARLENE,
    I AM WRITING YOU THIS LETTER BECAUSE I MISS YOU SO MUCH. THIS TOUR HAS BEEN ESPECIALLY HARD ON ME BECAUSE AFTER MAKING THE MOVIE I HAD SUCH A SMALL TIME TO BE WITH YOU. I REALLY FEEL AS THOUGH THE PAST YEAR WE HAVE BEEN SEPERATED. MENTALY IF NOT PHISICALY.
    MY LIFE HAS GONE THROUGH SO MANY DRAMATIC CHANGES IN THE PAST FEW YEARS SOMETIMES I AM SUPRISED I AM ALIVE. EVEN AT THIS MOMENT, ALTHOUGH I AM SURROUNDED BY PEOPLE. I AM EXTREMELY LONELY.
    UNTIL ICE WAS BORN, I WAS NEVER SO AWARE OF HOW MUCH I DEPEND AND NEED YOU BUT YOUR ATTENTION RIGHTFULLY WAS AIMED AT THE BABY AND I STARTED TO TRIP.
    NOW I TRULY REALIZE THAT MY WHOLE LIFE IS BUILT AROUND YOU AND MAKING YOU HAPPY AND SAFE. THE THOUGHT OF EVER LOSING YOU MAKES MY HEART STOP.
    I KNOW I HAVE NEVER WRITTEN YOU A LETTER. I ALSO NEVER USE TO CALL YOU TWICE A DAY EITHER!   →   ①

DEFINITION OF DOWN

FASSBIND HOTELS

Alle Zimmer unserer Hotels bieten Farbfernsehen mit Gratis-Videofilmen, Radio, Direktwahl-Telefon, Mini-Bar, Telefax und Computeranschluss. Nichtraucherzimmer.

BERN

HOTEL AMBASSADOR**
Seftigenstrasse 99
Tel. (031) 454 111
ab 23.09.93: 031/371 41 11
Fax (031) 454 117
ab 23.09.93: 031/371 41 17
Telex 911 826
Ruhige Lage.
Wunderschöne Aussicht auf das Bundeshaus.
Gratis-Parkplätze, Restaurant, Bar, Hallenschwimmbad.

LAUSANNE

HOTEL AGORA**
Tél. (021) 617 12 11

HOTEL ALPHA**
Tél. (021) 230 131
ab 14.09.93: 021/323 01 31

NEUES HOTEL CITY*
Tél. (021) 202 141
ab 14.09.93: 021/320 21 41

GENF

HOTEL CRISTAL**
Tél. (022) 731 34 00

LUGANO

HOTEL CONTINENTAL*
Tél. (091) 561 112

Kongresszentrum FH:
Bern   Hotel Ambassador
Lausanne   Hotel Agora
            Hotel Alpha

I KNOW THAT THE REST OF MY LIFE WILL BE SPENT WITH YOU GETTIN MORE AND MORE SEXY AS YOU STRIVE TO MAKE ME HAPPY. I IN RETURN WILL WORK MY HEART OUT TO PROVIDE FOR YOU AND LIL ICE.
 I LOVE YOU MORE THAN I EVER HAVE IN MY LIFE AND I KNOW THAT I NEED YOU AND WOULD DIE WITHOUT YOU.
 I'VE ALWAYS RUN FROM COMITMENT BECAUSE I HAVE NO FAMILY AND NEVER FELT STABEL. DARLENE YOU AND ICE ARE NOW MY FAMILY AND I WILL NO LONGER RUN.
 PLEASE TRY TO UNDERSTAND ME THOUGH I KNOW I'VE HURT YOU BEFORE, BUT I WILL NEVER LEAVE YOU AND WOULD DEFINIATLY DIE FOR YOU!
 GOD SENT YOU TO ME, BECAUSE YOU ARE TRULY MY ULTIMATE DREAM GIRL. I CAN'T WAIT HOLD YOU IN MY ARMS.
 TRUE LOVE
 TRACY   ③

watching the stars and talking for hours. I could listen to that man talk about anything. He was just so interesting, witty and charming. The downside was I was going through an insecure phase. I'd lost most of the baby weight three months after I gave birth but I was still feeling flabby. I felt like I wasn't up to my own toned and tight standards yet.

One night, while we were staring at the stars, I summoned up the courage to offer him what I thought an international superstar would want. I thought I wouldn't be enough for him anymore so I said: "Hey, we're here in Mexico, away from people we know. We could go back to that nightclub we went to last night and ask one of the women..."

He cut me off before I could even spit it out. I figured a rock star fantasy would include a three-way and made the offer because I knew I had changed because of motherhood, and I wanted him to be happy.

He said: "Hell, no, D! I don't need any of that. You are more than enough woman for me."

I said: "But, baby, you always hear about rock stars and what they get up to."

And he said, "Yeah, but what you don't hear is how badly those things end."

He told me guys who do that don't do it with women they love, because it always destroys the relationship.

What I couldn't figure is whether or not he was ruling a three-way out on principle or ruling it out with me involved. I didn't know where this was going or what it actually meant, but I was off the hook.

The next night when we went back to the nightclub, you should have seen the smiles on our faces. We were having a good time, the two of us together. I think he was proud of me, he knew how much I loved him and I think it was special to him that I was willing to put myself out there like that.

DEFINITION OF DOWN

I came back feeling wonderful. He made me feel beautiful, and I got my confidence back.

* * * * * *

By entertainment industry standards, we were considered a traditional family.

And leave it to Tracy to move us on up to an even bigger, better, higher Hollywood Hills home.

I could've lived in a teepee with him, but I never questioned his desire to want more. He had that itch to have his home reflect his success, and he didn't think our Bogie bungalow was big enough.

Lil Ice was about seven months old when Tracy called me all excited. "I found the home!" he said. "It's perfect! It's not a poor man's view." He was quoting our realtor, who explained a poor man's view was a view of the valley. "This is the real thing!" Tracy continued. "You can see the ocean, downtown, all the way to Catalina Island on a clear day."

First thing I asked was, "Does it have a pool?"

He said, "Nope! But I'll build one."

And he sure did. We got into a bidding war with Scott Hamilton, the ice skater, but Tracy's stubbornness prevailed.

"That lil dude don't know what to do with a house like this," he said.

Our nearest neighbor was the football player Jim Brown, and Tracy was so amped up because as a teen he went to parties at Brown's home and now here he was, buying in the neighborhood, even higher up the hill.

When I first saw the house, I thought, Sweet! It's brand new, ready to move in.

Tracy called me into the master bedroom to show me the walk-in closet. I laid down in the closet in awe. It was bigger than our first apartment.

I told him, "It's perfect. When are we moving in?"

And that's when Antoine popped up. I can still see his face, thinking, pondering, envisioning just exactly what he was going to tear up.

The gorgeous hardwood floors were the first to go. In their place, black marble flooring to match the black marble countertops in the kitchen. Again, he added a drop-down movie screen in the living room. He also added chrome baseboards. He replaced the wooden handrails with chrome. He designed and added two aquariums, one was a shark tank that he had to install with a crane. Eventually, he added a pool with a retractable roof and walls, so it could be indoor or outdoor.

He added a recording studio with a mixing board that was so huge it had to be installed with a crane as well. To make it fit, he had to have workers cut a huge hole into the side of the home and swing it through.

We didn't make any friends with the Beverly Hills Homeowners Association, who were looking up at our construction project trying to figure out ways to halt it. Tracy would point out there's no homeowner's association at the top of the hill, and he just kept building whatever his heart desired.

He also did right by our son by spending thousands of dollars to baby proof the home, including adding plexiglass to the railings that surrounded the exterior of the house.

Antoine's touches were everywhere. The house was filled out with black carpeting and his Asian touches, like the Ming temple dogs that he placed in front of our home that were supposed to protect the home from evil. Instead, someone pilfered them almost immediately. Tracy was so upset, but we went right back down to Chinatown and got two more, which he then cemented into the pavement near the front door.

DEFINITION OF DOWN

He was excited about having his own studio to record in. The idea of producing his next album in his own recording studio was the fulfillment of a lifelong dream.

Unfortunately, it wasn't our neighbor's dream. Little did we know, the neighbor to our left had serious problems of his own. He'd get drunk and start screaming in front of his house, "I got Jews to the left of me! Niggas to the right! This world is coming to an end!"

Tracy would laugh, watching him on our security cameras. "Look at this fool!" he'd say, showing us the guy on camera. We knew he had a problem, we just didn't know how serious it was. Shortly thereafter, he died of AIDS. And eventually, one of the film producers who worked with Dr. Dre moved in and we're like, "Alriiight, now the neighborhood is getting some flavor."

Before we got off that block, our neighbors included J.C. Chasez from NSYNC, Justin Timberlake, Britney Spears, Mark McGrath from Sugar Ray, and Fred Durst from Limp Bizkit. Oh, yeah, there went the neighborhood.

12 DRAMA

Suddenly, Tracy was front page news. But it wasn't from a film role. It was courtesy of Dan Quayle and Charlton Heston, two unlikely speed metal fans. Because even though they continued to refer to the infamous "Cop Killer" record as a rap song, we knew better.

Everything that can possibly be said about that song has already been said, but the bottom line is if you lived that scandal firsthand during that time, it was scary.

I knew Tracy would never let anyone hurt us over his art, but I could see the toll it was taking on him when the controversy hit full speed. He was undermined by a bunch of people who never even listened to his music.

The record had already been out for a long time before it hit the headlines. It was a protest song that dealt with police brutality, which was rampant at the time in Los Angeles. It also foreshadowed the riots of 1992.

We were driving back from Beverly Hills one day, and somehow, we got caught in the foot traffic of the Warner Bros. shareholders meeting, where protestors happened to be crossing the streets. They weren't dressed as cops, but we found out later they were cops. That was the meeting where Charlton Heston, the president of the NRA, quoted from the song's lyrics.

Tracy couldn't believe our luck. Our car was right in the thick of it. We were stopped at a red light, in a Rolls Royce no less, with a license plate that read: PIPN8EZ (pimpin' ain't easy). And the protestors started to crane their necks. When they realized who he was, they started cursing and yelling obscenities. Right before the light turned green, Tracy rolled his window down and flipped off the crowd and said, "I'm with my family!"

Before we even made it back up the hill, that picture was on the news. This is long before social media so someone sure acted fast, but his feeling was he had his family with him and they were infringing on our rights. We just happened to land in the wrong place at the wrong time.

I was really worried for him. Not only did I take all the death threats we received seriously, but I could see it was tearing him up inside. That shitstorm was brewing big time.

He didn't sleep. He lost weight. He took responsibility for the impact it was having on the people he worked with at Warner Bros. He didn't want them to have to suffer for his artistic expression. So he decided to pull the plug.

He held a press conference and said he was removing himself from the label. His record sales had been a big part of Warner Bros.'s success during this period and it was a sad day for everyone.

Needless to say, the controversy generated even bigger record sales and another tour. But this time, not just his fans would show up. We also got our fair share of protestors.

I remember being in Chicago, it was freezing cold, we had Lil Ice with us, and protestors would mob our bus. It was such a trip. We'd park as close as we could to each venue, and then we would have to make a run for it. I remember handing Lil Ice to one of the Body Count musicians, Mooseman, to put under his jacket, because we had no idea what the protestors might do. And this happened in the majority of the bigger cities.

It was such a crazy time, and my family was fearful for us. But just like we did everything, we handled it together. And we weathered it and got through it.

As soon as they didn't have the Warner Bros. shareholders to scare anymore, the controversy died down and we went on with our life.

But true to form, Tracy had to have the last word and he did it with the first video off his next rap record, *Home Invasion*. The song "I Ain't New Ta This" opens with actors playing cops, teasing him about being broke since he parted ways with Warner Bros., and then it goes right to Tracy's boat, *Rated X*, where he proceeds to say this ain't nothing new to him.

I'll never forget that shoot. I was still getting my groove back after having our son when we got a knock at the door. We were filming some of the parts at our house, and two actresses showed up that Tracy had hired for the day. I wasn't expecting that. What the hell?! I told one of Tracy's boys, "Um, some girls are here."

I could hear Tracy yell up, "Tell Darlene to take care of them."

I'm never one to start any drama, so I kept it professional. I took them upstairs and helped them with their bags.

This was some new shit. You can only imagine what was going through my head because I'd always been the girl in the video. It was just a given. He'd never needed to hire outside help before. But whatever. There I was with the kid on my hip, helping these two young women get ready for the shoot.

I remember seething inside, because he could always talk to me about anything, and I felt like this was a big betrayal. For it to go down like that was a first.

About an hour later, I was minding my own business in Lil Ice's room, when I get a knock on the door.

It was one of Tracy's boys again. "Um, Darlene, Tracy wants to talk to you."

DEFINITION OF DOWN

So I feigned concern, like I gave a shit.

"Omigawd! What's wrong?"

"We got a little bit of a situation, and Tracy needs your help."

"For real?! What you need me for?"

I'm still licking my wounds, but I'm not letting anyone else see it. I played that off.

Tracy starts stuttering; he was having a tough time getting it out. But apparently, the actresses reneged on their roles. They didn't realize what it would entail, i.e., shaking their asses in bathing suits, with Tracy rubbing oil on them.

So, of course, he turns to old faithful, ol' reliable, after he tried to push me to the curb. But once again, I got his back. Dammit, I'm thinking, I wasn't even in prime shape, but I handled my business.

I gave Lil Ice off to one of his boys, dusted off my thong and my heels, found some baby oil and shook my hair loose and said, "Where do I go?"

I look back at the video now and realize I held it down. I did the damn thing once again.

13

99 PROBLEMS & D AIN'T ONE

Even in the earliest days of our relationship, there were signs of other women.

That first trip to New York, I'd found some photos. I asked him, "Oh, who's this?" And he got all defensive. "Oh, D! Come on. You've got to get used to this. She's posing with everybody."

He made me feel embarrassed for even asking, and it got me thinking that maybe I was just being insecure.

I genuinely felt bad for even asking. But in the back of my mind I thought, damn, he sure got defensive. I was still a teenager when that happened, but as I got older, I saw more of what was going on.

Any time I questioned him about anything, though, he always let me know how much he loved me. And as his fame grew, I figured it was natural for other women to desire him. Over the years, I'd find random photos of girls, phone numbers, letters and even undeveloped film. I kept it all in a bag that a Power Rangers baby quilt came in, knowing he'd never look there.

I knew my mother role had changed the dynamic of our relationship. That's just how it was.

We've already established the freewheeling rock 'n' roll lifestyle changes when you become a parent, but some people don't want to change with it. While I was intent on being a good mom and creating a

DEFINITION OF DOWN

wonderful home for our child, he was becoming, for lack of a better word, a ho. But just like the song by dancehall artist Shaggy, he'd say, "It wasn't me." He never fessed up to his indiscretions.

His denials were hilarious. Right out of the player handbook.

I could've caught him in bed with a woman, and he still would've denied she was even there. He would've told me I was delusional.

The stories he concocted to explain the plethora of ho's who left a trail were really quite clever. He'd say: "D, you're trippin', making something out of nothing. Do women come up here looking for me? Do they call the house? No! That's because there's nothing going on."

Denied it right down to the bitter end.

I had all kinds of evidence: explicit pictures, letters, magazine layouts. I'd even see him driving around in his car with other women.

He'd say, "Oh, that's just so-and-so's secretary. I had to give the bitch a ride."

Tough to fight that.

For some reason, I'd see him out everywhere. Even in this big ol' town, we'd run into each other in the most random places. One time, I was taking Lil Ice to karate practice, and who pulled up next to us at the stop? His dad with another woman in the car. Even Lil Ice said, "Who's he with? Why didn't he stop and say hi?"

What am I supposed to say?

The pictures were the best of the tour ho's. The women sitting on his bed in hotels with the backstage pass on and the eloquent refrain printed: "No Head, No Backstage Pass."

I still have the nasty magazine that a friend's boyfriend gave to me, concerned for me. It featured a layout with the headline: "Meet Ice T's New Ho."

Yeah, that was the stripper, and the magazine was the lowest of the low. You could see the bullet wounds, scars, you could even see what STDs these broads had. Then there was that actress, who was a well-known ho. And don't forget the one who wrote the book, the really nasty one; that was a real low point. Oh, yeah, then there's the one he knocked up.

I always wanted more children and he was so set against it. When one of his groupies turned up pregnant later, it was definitely salt on the wound.

It was so not who he used to be. He was always proud of the fact that he didn't have a bunch of kids from a bunch of women, and he used to say so. He was proud of the fact that he wasn't giving his money away to groupies, like a lot of his other peers. Unfortunately, that would change.

But I never dwelled on his indiscretions. If anything, when he fucked up he could be even sweeter. He didn't throw it in my face. At least at the beginning he didn't.

I knew other women came with the territory of superstardom. It takes a really strong person to not succumb to temptation, and truly, women are everywhere when you're touring and on film sets.

But it got to the point where his affairs started to break me down. The first six years of our relationship, we were so tight. It was pure bliss and no one in this universe was happier than we were. I know that in my heart to be true.

But even as he would hide the affairs from me, it wasn't long before there was no place to hide because he was so prolific, the women did start showing up in uninvited places.

DEFINITION OF DOWN

One woman even followed us on a cruise ship to Mexico. Tracy and I were checking in on the cruise line and I noticed a women in sunglasses who kept staring at us. It wasn't like, "Oh! That's Ice T and Darlene!" It was a more sinister look, like she was mad-dogging us.

We got on the boat, and this woman followed us everywhere. I asked him, "What the hell is going on with this broad?"

He got defensive and told me I was just imagining things.

But then we hit our first stop on Catalina Island. And she was still following us, trying to squeeze onto the same little transport boat with us. He was trying so hard to ignore her, but she kept mad-dogging me.

Suddenly, she confronted him and then he stormed off and next thing I know I hear her saying, "Forget you, Tracy!" And then before I know it, he starts arguing with me and tells me to forget it. I've got tears streaming down my face and then all hell starts breaking loose.

Instead of just apologizing to me, he starts turning on the charm. He gave me some cockamamie story about her being some broad that tried to get with him, and now she wants to take it out on us. We finished the cruise, but it was another wedge between us.

It got to a point where I had to make a decision to not go out in public with him as much anymore. It was clear to me, somewhere along the line his shit was getting out of fuckin' hand because the incidents were becoming more frequent and more disrespectful.

One night, he got us tickets to MC Lyte, who he knew I loved. It was at the Mayan Theatre in downtown L.A. and I was hesitant. I didn't want any scenes. My heart couldn't handle it. It wasn't like the good old days, where we'd be cheesing ear to ear. There was tension because you never knew which broad would come out of the woodwork.

He was genuinely upset that we didn't go out as much. He'd invite me everywhere, but I was making excuses for obvious reasons. We had a family to keep intact.

I knew he really wanted me to go with him to the show, and so I reluctantly agreed. But I had a bad feeling about this night and sho' nuff: drama.

We were at the concert, and we were seated at a table with other friends. My bad feeling kept me from relaxing, and when a crowd of women walked by, something was said. I didn't hear what it was, but Tracy's friends jumped up and went and handled it.

Something not good was unfolding and here we go again. I could feel it.

DEFINITION OF DOWN

I played it off like usual, and when a good song came on, I said, "Let's dance."

We went out on the dance floor and it was crowded, and I noticed that some of the women from that same group were dancing awfully close to us. Tracy ignored them, but when some broad starts tapping his shoulder, it got pretty obvious.

"Tracy, this girl is behind you tapping you hello. Are you gonna respond?" I said.

He turned around and they started getting in each other's face and suddenly you got two crews confronting each other and I heard him say, "What the fuck are you doing? Can't you see I'm out here with my girl?"

Her girls started pulling her away and Tracy's boys started crowding around him, protecting him.

As she's being pulled away, I hear her say, "Fuck you, Tracy!" And I'm thinking, this is exactly why I didn't want to go out.

What people need to understand is this kinda shit is dangerous. People get shot for less, and here is a situation where no one's safe and you're messing with people's emotions. She didn't give a shit he was with me, and I just wanted to get the hell out of there. I was humiliated, once again.

We got in the car, and our friend Evil E was with us. You could just feel the tension. No one said a single word, and we dropped Evil off at his home. I had a sinking feeling Tracy was going to try to ignore what had just happened and try to play it off, once again.

I wasn't about to ignore this one. It had crossed the line, and I wanted to hold him accountable. I decided to play him. It was out of my character because I was so cool when shit would go down. I was his girl and I stood by him always, but this was a perfect moment for me to confront and challenge him because now it was public. We had witnesses.

"So I don't have any women calling me out, showing up where we are and creating drama, huh? What do you call that?" I said.

He couldn't handle it because I'd never challenged him like that before. I couldn't help it, I gave him back his own shit. "You can't brush this one off, Tracy. Your mess is now on my doorstep..."

All I know is I was still talking when I felt the smack in my face, and my head hit the passenger window. I lost it.

He had never hit me before, and he always said if he ever got that heated he would just walk away. Here we were in a car and he couldn't walk away. He clearly had a guilty conscience. His shit was getting sloppier and sloppier. And at that moment, he took it out on me.

I'm screaming because it was the last thing expected from this guy, who'd always been so chill and so cool.

"Let me out of this fucking car!" I screamed.

He kept telling me to calm down but I wasn't calm, and as soon as he came to a stop, I flew out of that car.

I was in Echo Park in five-inch stilettos and a short skirt, and I didn't give a fuck. I didn't have a cell phone, and I was just about to knock on a stranger's door when Tracy called out to me, "D, get in the car."

The first thing I thought about was his career. How lame is that. I was so fucking loyal to him that I'm worried about his career and how something like this would affect it.

I walked out of that stranger's yard and kept walking.

He wouldn't give up and wasn't about to leave me there. I could see that even he looked frightened about what had just happened. He didn't try to play it off either, he just kept pleading for me to get back in the car.

I finally got in the car, and he apologized. He said, "D, I'm sorry..." He kept rambling on, and I didn't hear his words. "Wa... wa... wa..."

I had been with him since I was 17 years old, we had a child together, and I didn't know who this guy was anymore. He had never been physical and it triggered a flood of memories. Rose, who I fought off my whole childhood until I met my rescue hero. This wonderful man, Tracy Marrow.

What the fuck?! Shit was catching up with him, and it was destroying us slowly. He took me home that night, after spinning some long-winded yarn about how it wasn't what it seemed, but he looked me in the eye and promised me he'd never ever lay a hand on me again.

True to his word, he never did.

The next incident that happened where he got angry for getting caught again, he just stomped out, got in his car and left.

Imagine what would've happened if social media was around then. All these incidents would've been caught on video. I often wonder how long we would have been able to withstand that kind of scrutiny. I feel terrible for famous couples now, because they don't have a chance of any normalcy.

But something definitely changed after that night. I don't know if he tightened up his game or if he simply stopped ho'ing around, but there was a noticeable decline in events like those.

I, for one, was grateful, because I didn't need that kind of drama.

I look at him today and think, boy, he's got his work cut out for him cuz nowadays, these ho's are tough to keep in check.

They don't make 'em like me anymore.

14 THE RAIN

I tried so hard to make our marriage work because that's really what we had: we had a marriage. No paper, but we were together through thick and thin. I have so much happiness in my heart when I look back at the early days, just sheer joy at where we started and what we accomplished together as a team.

The letters say it all.

> DARLENE,
> I JUST ARRIVED IN LONDON AND HAVE TO DO SOME INTERVIEWS BEFORE THE SHOW TONIGHT. I REALLY ENJOYED TALKING TO YOU LAST NIGHT, BUT I'M SORRY I WOKE YOU UP (I KNOW HOW YOU ARE ABOUT YOUR SLEEP!!!)
> IF I COULD HAVE ONE WISH, I WOULD WISH TO BE WITH YOU ALWAYS. I'M TIRED OF BEING AWAY FROM YOU AND LIL ICE, BUT I KNOW THAT A REAL MAN HAS TO GO OUT AND GET THE MONEY TO SUPPORT HIS FAMILY TO THE STANDARDS HE HAS SET FOR THEM -NO MATTER WHAT! SO THAT MEANS YOU AND ICE ARE ONLY GONNA HAVE THE VERY- VERY BEST!!! THATS MY JOB FOR THE REST OF MY LIFE.
> HAVE A GOOD DAY AND GET STARTED ON THAT SHOPPING SPREE!!!! YOU BETTER HAVE A GANG OF NEW THINGS TO SHOW ME WHEN I GET HOME OR I'LL BE REALLY MAD! HA HA!!   LOVE   TRAY   TAG

But when it started to break bad, it got really bad, and then down came the rain.

I am a joyful person. I always try to look on the sunny side of life, and I so wanted our son to have a happy childhood. Tracy gave me the gift of being a stay-at-home mom. He wanted me to be the best at it, but at the same time, it gave him opportunity. I was holding down the fort while this fool starts living the single life.

He'd lost his mind. And when that rain came down, it just kept coming.

The deterioration of our relationship happened in phases, and a lot of it had to do with power. We'd spend less and less time together, even though we made a mighty effort at the beginning of motherhood. But he had less control and needed undivided attention. And to regain his sense of power, I guess he needed attention from other women, a lot of other women.

What did he think? That I would be the lil wifey at home, while he's out acting like he's single? That's not a player move. That's weak to me. Rather than say, "Hey, look, this is the direction I'm going in, and I don't want to hurt you." But instead, he played all those mind games, and it tore up my heart. It's just so sick and twisted. I tried to retaliate by seeing other men. He was gone so much, and I was incredibly lonely, but it just never felt right. He'd even tell me that he'd understand if I took up with a male friend for company, as long as I never threw it in his face and as long as I never left him or fell in love with anyone else.

The bottom line: I loved him and wanted to be with only him.

* * * * * *

I'll never forget one moment in time. It was right after New Year's in the early 2000s. Tracy was sitting with our son watching TV. By then, he had a major part in *Law & Order: SVU* and had been commuting back and forth from New York to L.A. A commercial came on with two elderly people on the screen. "That's going to be me and your mom," he said to Lil Ice. I remember thinking, "What a sweet thing to say." Unfortunately, our Hip Hop fairytale would come to an end just four months later, when he broke up with me over a two-way pager. After 17 years, I get a breakup text. Well, several pages of a breakup text.

It's not like I didn't see it coming. His moves were getting shabbier.

Just a few months earlier, I'd picked him up from the airport, and I felt a huge shift in his behavior. No matter what we'd been through, every time we'd see each other, it was always still exciting. He'd call me every second and ask me what I was wearing and tell me how much he couldn't wait to see me. But this time was different. He couldn't look me in the eye. And then I noticed his baggage tags said "Arizona." I looked at him and said, "Arizona, again?" He said, "Oh, yeah, I'm trying to get this role. I had to go talk to this guy."

I just thought, Whatever, but I could sense a distance between us. We got in the car, he always wanted to drive. I'd been listening to KJLH, and a Ginuwine song came on. He said, "Ooh ooh, turn this up! I love this song!" I thought, when the hell did he ever listen to current R&B love ballads? He started singing the lyrics, "My whole life has changed, since you came in, I knew back then you were that special one... " I literally had my head turned looking at him like, "What the hell is this?" He was somewhere else. And there it was. I knew we were at the edge of the cliff.

His next visit would be our last, the last in that home, together as a family.

Ice and I picked him from LAX, and there again, I noticed the Arizona baggage tags. I didn't say anything this time. I didn't think it was worth it. It was the holidays of 2001. He said he was really tired. I'd just gotten certified as a massage therapist, and he said he was looking forward to being my first client.

Lil Ice was in the backseat all excited to see his dad and telling him how we'd set up the massage table upstairs for him.

We got to the house and took his bags in and he plopped down on the massage table. Lil Ice was watching TV, smiling away at us, happy to see his parents together. I gave Tracy a massage, and as he was lying there, we hear him start to snore. Lil Ice and I started giggling, and then all of a sudden, the happy moment was interrupted by the sound of a loud buzzing. It was his two-way

DEFINITION OF DOWN

pager on the nightstand, and it was blowing up.

Lil Ice, being as innocent as he was, said, "Mom! You better stop that! It'll wake up dad!" I grabbed the pager, opened it up and there it was. A message from a woman which read: "I really wish you'd change your mind and come back here for the holidays. I hate to spend New Year's Eve alone. I understand you have your obligations, but I want you here."

Lil Ice said, "Mom, who was it?"

I said, "Oh, it's nothing." I closed it quickly. I put face on for my kid and was about to go back toward Tracy, when all of a sudden, I hear Lil Ice let out a scream.

"Mom! Something's coming out of dad's bag!"

I looked closer and saw a white scorpion crawling out of Tracy's suitcase. No joke! By then Tracy woke up and saw what was going on, grabbed a shoe and pressed it down on top of the scorpion.

He said, "You gotta be kidding me. Where'd that come from?"

"It crawled out of your bag!" I said.

He shooed it outside and we watched it walk around on our balcony with its tail up. It was the creepiest thing. We all were stunned, not saying anything for a long time.

I couldn't help but think it was a bad omen.

* * * * * *

We were getting ready for the holidays and New Year's Eve was approaching. And sure enough, two days before New Year's Eve, he sprung it on us.

"Yeah, D, I got a gig for New Year's. I'm gonna get paid, and I should go," he said.

The kid was bummed, but he knew I'd snuck up a bunch of illegal fireworks from Tijuana. He shrugged his shoulders and told his dad, "Too bad you're gonna miss the fireworks."

I felt sick to my stomach because I knew Tracy was lying, and it was like playing out the longest death scene ever. I looked at him like, "Really?! You're gonna do this to us..."

"Yeah, the car's on its way now."

In my heart of hearts, I knew this was the end.

When the Town Car came, Lil Ice started to cry and Tracy gave me a hug. Whenever he would leave us, he used to always leave happy and upbeat, but this time he just looked sad, defeated. He turned around and looked at us until we were out of view.

That was the last time I saw him for two years.

* * * * * *

I was at the Hollywood YMCA getting my certification as a spin instructor the next morning, and I couldn't ignore how I was feeling.

I sent Tracy a message, "We really need to talk."

He hit me back, "Okay. I know when you say that, it's not good. Call me when you can."

As soon as I got out of the class, I looked at my pager and there were five messages from him. I thought, "Oh, look at this bullshit. Are you kidding me?!"

It read, "D, I know what you're getting ready to say, but it's not what you're thinking..." And there it was, a long drawn out Dear

DEFINITION OF DOWN

John letter on why we needed to part. He said he was never coming back to L.A. That shocked me. It was so surreal because we had a kid here in L.A.

He told me it had nothing to do with another woman, that there was no one good enough to be around his son, and he was taking a break from a lot of things.

Why couldn't he tell me the truth? It would have made things so much easier. It would sting, but I'd respect him more in the end.

I started hearing about him being with another woman within days of us breaking up. No one even knew we'd broken up, because I didn't broadcast it. But people were asking me, "What's up with T and that broad?"

For a guy who didn't believe in marriage, he didn't waste any time marrying Ol' Gal.

* * * * * *

He was a player till the end. He never copped to another relationship.

Subj: LETTER
Date: Thursday, January 10, 2002 9:21:01 AM
From: TLM007
To: DM0007

Dear Darlene,
Since my last message to you I've taken time out to think.. The reason I prefer to write is so I have the time to read and make sure the words I say are correct.
After telling you that I think we should live our own lives, I can't lie I felt a great pain. You have been a tremendous woman to me over the years & the most incredible mother to my son... I want you to know that the moves I felt I had to make and say, was just an attempt to remove a lot of the lies from our relationship so that maybe & hopefully we will never become ugly and enemies...
The truth is for the past years we have moved farther and farther apart... I have absolutely no doubt that you love me..... Things have just changed.
I'll try to explain how I feel...
Right now in my life I *have to feel* like all of my options are open.. I don't know where I want to live. What I want to do. Or who I want to be with. Honestly I found out the least stress for me was to be alone. Sure every girl I meet wants to try to hold me down but that's where the stress comes from the gate. People *depending* on me. Of course anyone I meet is gonna say they love me.... I'm a nice guy & seem to be well off. The *truth* is I am terrified by any form of commitment... It will always end up in me pulling the weight. It always has...You've been a perfect woman and I'm loosing it so I know someone else is not gonna make me feel better.
Although I've been actually living a simulated singles life I am aware of the lie we're living.. Once again - I do not doubt our love for each other. I just feel that if it *is* really true. It's time to get it real.
I don't want to live my life freely and have you afraid to live yours because you fear that I will trip out and try and make you leave from the house or anything.

I truly don't know what *you* want but this is what I would like to happen.
No matter what.. I'm gonna keep paying the house note and the bills at the house & supporting you and Ice. That house was for you and Ice to live in and

DEFINITION OF DOWN

you will, until YOU feel otherwise. Actually nothing in LA has to change at all... I'm just letting you know that you are entitled to live..... If you meet another man and fall in love... Then I'll have to except that. I think we can still be close and talk. I think you can still help me in LA.. I need it.
I think we can still keep Ice happy! It's all how we handle this situation. Ice has never seen me with another woman... He's with you so that's something you'll have to consider.. As far as you and other people.. If we stay fly. This dose not have to ever get ugly.
I just don't know my next move and you should know that. That's respect..
I'm just trying to be honest with you and myself so that I can readjust my life and get some mental peace. In order to do that I have to *for once and for all* say what's truly on my mind & in my heart... I'm not doing this to try to hurt you. I'm just trying to level with myself.
I guess it's as simple as this,
I'm sick of LA.. The drama I left there was very obvious. So I don't wanna come back there to live anymore.
We don't have to tell each other what we're doing ... But we don't have to lie and say we're doing nothing..
We have a beautiful son... We'll always be together in some way. We gotta keep it fly. For him at least.
You may decide to go left and sue me.. Who knows?
I may regret this the rest of my life... But right now it's what i feel I have to do to get my head straight...   love tracy

PS. I went to a doctor out here.. I have an Ulcer. I'm going into the hospital this weekend.
PSS. I didn't tell you that for any sympathy. I just felt you should know.

15

DEFINITION OF DOWN

Valentine's Day hit me haaaard. It was nearly two months since we'd broken up and Tracy's birthday fell on February 16 and we always celebrated big. We'd usually go to Teena Marie's Valentine's Day shows together.

She was playing at the House of Blues that year, and she'd given me four front row balcony seats. I brought a friend, who tried to set me up with a date. Poor guy. I didn't say two words to him. I always make fun of people who wear sunglasses at night, but that night, I was one of them. I'd been crying all day, and I knew when Teena started singing–especially "Casanova Brown"–I'd lose it.

From that night on, people started asking what happened with me and Tracy. When I told them we were no longer together, no one believed me. Teena actually got angry. So many people were shocked because they thought of us as this iconic couple. I used to say, "Who are you tellin'? I'm as surprised as you."

I didn't realize how sad I must have looked, because a friend of mine took me aside one day and said, "Look, D, we gotta go see Grandma." I had no idea what that meant but he told me, "I can see how bad you're hurtin' and I think she can help you."

As we drove to visit his grandmother, he explained to me, "Grandma has sight."

I'm sure I looked shocked.

DEFINITION OF DOWN

He said, "Don't be scared. This might help you deal with a few things."

I'd never met her before. We walked into her home, which was in deep South Central. She was in her late 70s or early 80s. She was wearing a muumuu, and it appeared that she was confined to her bed. As soon as I sat next to her, I got a very comforting feeling. She took my hand and she just held it for awhile.

"You're a friend of my grandson," she said.

"Yes," I told her.

She nodded and asked me to hand her the deck of cards on her nightstand. She told me to shuffle them and to then make three stacks.

She pulled a card from the top of the center stack and turned it over. It was the queen of hearts. "This is you," she said.

She started going through the cards and reading them. She began telling me about my life and my future. She told me I would be financially okay and that I was going to go on a trip soon. She also told me I was going to find money. My face didn't give anything away but I was terribly worried that Tracy wouldn't take care of us financially anymore and her words were reassuring. I was also going on a trip to Las Vegas later that month, and true to her words, I found a mound of crispy hundred dollar bills while cleaning out Tracy's junk drawer a week later.

As she finished reading the cards, she looked at me and said, "About your son's dad, it's like he's dead to you."

Her words gave me chills. I hadn't expressed those feelings to anyone, but that's exactly how I felt. He was there one day, and then he was gone. No phone calls, no checking up on us. He truly felt dead to me. I squeezed her hand so hard.

And then out of nowhere, she said, "The woman who is with him now with the colored eyes is only with him for his money."

That put another chill down my spine.

She then asked me if there's anything else I wanted to know about him, if I wanted to know how he passes.

I told her, "No, oh, definitely not."

She started to tell me about his stomach problems and how sick he was and how he needed to take care of that. She was dead on about that as well. Tracy had an ulcer that had plagued him for years. A month later, he was in the hospitable getting an operation to deal with his chronic stomach pain.

I went back two more times to see her, and each time, I learned more and realized through her sight I was able to summon more strength to move on.

But ultimately, my conversations with God and keeping my faith made me realize everything was going to be alright. I began to tell my family about our breakup. I'd kept it inside, because I was still dealing with it myself.

I hadn't told Lil Ice, because I had hoped Tracy would fly out and we could tell him together. As the weeks went by, it was clear that wasn't going to happen, and I just couldn't look at that little face anymore. He kept asking where his dad was.

I had to tell him.

* * * * * *

Family has always been so very important to me, and I never wanted to do Tracy dirty. He'd been my man for so long, and despite the rain, I'd always love him.

I ain't gonna lie. It was tough to lose him. I was still dealing with

DEFINITION OF DOWN

the loss of my beautiful father, Pete, who'd been diagnosed with lung cancer. Those of you who think weed won't kill you might want to rethink that. My pops smoked weed for 35 years, and his lungs were charred black when his time came. True to the O.G. he was, Pete wanted to go out on his own terms. He didn't want to be shot up with chemicals, and he didn't want the agony prolonged. He was angry about how Dr. Kevorkian was treated, because he believed people should have the right to choose death if they are diagnosed with a terminal illness and if they're in pain.

Pete didn't want to wait until he was ravaged, but even as death closed in, he was still my beautiful father. I was there when he died. He wanted to die in his childhood home, and the two of us were watching NASCAR together. I told him I was going to take a shower and asked him if it would be okay. He said, "Go ahead, mija."

I got up to leave the room, and I turned around to look at him. I watched him slowly cross his hands over his chest as if preparing for death.

I started to walk back toward him and he said, "Go, mija. I'm okay."

The next thing I knew, my grandmother was banging on the shower door, crying.

"He's gone, mija! He's gone!"

When I came back into his room, Lil Ice was at his bedside with my grandparents. It was agonizing watching my grandmother mourn the loss of her firstborn child. Pete looked so peaceful, and every day of my life, I am grateful to have had such a wonderful father.

* * * * * *

Rose, on the other hand, didn't have such a peaceful departure from this planet. I'd been estranged from her for years. The funny thing is, you think someone like Rose is gonna live forever. But I got a call from one of my sisters telling me she was in a diabetic coma from her drinking and could I get to the hospital before they removed her life support.

I had mixed feelings about going to see her. I don't really have a place in my heart for her, other than an occasional sense of pity. I'd learned a few unpleasant things about her childhood over the years and none of it surprised me, but it did explain some of her behavior.

I told Lil Ice that I was going to the hospital and he said he wanted to come with me. He wanted to tell her how he felt.

When we got there, the doctor said she'd be able to hear his words, but she wouldn't be able to respond. Her hospital room had about 20 relatives crowded into it. Lil Ice hadn't met any of them.

He went up to Rose and said, "Grandma, hi, this is Lil Ice. I just wanted to say, it's really too bad you never got yourself together. You had three grandchildren and some amazing daughters..."

As soon as he started talking, her eyes welled up and her arm lifted up and everyone in the room gasped.

He continued: "You see what drinking does. You see how much you lost? You had all this time..." He just shook his head.

One of my aunts gave him a hug. And he came up to me, and I held him for a moment. His words were true.

They removed her life support, and I went back the next day. She was still in the room, and as I sat next to her, I witnessed her open her eyes and start thrashing her arms, gasping in a fearful manner. She had sheer terror on her face. My sister and I witnessed this together, and it was pretty scary.

Later that night, my sister called me and said, "Rose is gone."

DEFINITION OF DOWN

I asked how it happened.

She said Rose had another one of those spells, where it looked like she was fighting a demon. My sister said: "Girl, put it this way, it looked like Rose didn't want to go where she was going."

Hell's Bells. She's probably in some dive bar talking smack about my book. Rosie, I hope you shut the motherfucker down. You was one badass broad. Bottom line is, I survived.

* * * * * *

If there's one thing I can say about being Rose's daughter it's that I knew all about surviving. Even as a little girl, I'd take off and find a place of refuge. One of my favorite spots was a ditch, not far from the house. I'd bring my transistor radio and just lay down and look up at the stars. When it was cold, I'd find a spot in the laundry room of our apartment building. I'd cozy up next to a dryer and just chill.

Being self-sufficient kept me from suing Tracy for child support after we were through. It was more important to me that he have a good relationship with our son. And because I require very little to live happily, simplicity is the way for me. I always thought about his career first, and I knew how thin he was stretched. I'd kept his books for years, and he was providing for so many people. I stopped counting after he'd loaned out more than a million dollars. That's just who he was. I never wanted to add to any of his worries.

I made a nice home for Lil Ice and me in a two-bedroom apartment in Mid-City. It wasn't easy on our son but we managed. I never let our son see me be affectionate with another man, ever. That kid has so much to deal with on his dad's end that I felt it would have destroyed him. It's bad enough his dad was spending the time he should have spent with his son on another woman. It's a parent's moral obligation to do what's best for their children first. When you have a kid, it's no longer about you, and I think it's truly sad that so many men and women are about themselves first before their kids. You can never get those childhood years back. I'm thankful because my son has the utmost respect for me, and that's something you can't buy.

Two years ago, the small monthly checks Tracy would send stopped coming without any notice. I had just talked to him the week before, and we had a great conversation. He even talked about getting me on a reality show he was starring in. It was the best conversation we'd had in years, and I felt great about it.

Just a few days later, however, shit hit the fan in his personal life in a very public way. It had nothing to do with me, and I sure felt bad for him. I was very familiar with that kind of pain, and even though he was the cause of it in my life, I didn't wish it on him. I wouldn't wish it on anybody. And it was right after that incident that he cut me off. I find it so odd that people can take their pain out on the wrong person.

I had been working as a fitness instructor at the YMCA, doing a radio show with comedian Corey Holcomb, and each month, I would stretch Tracy's check as far as I could. Without it, I was in a spot.

I had hoped to be financially independent by then. A couple of years earlier, I'd asked Tracy for a small loan to start my own fitness studio, a little spot in South L.A. or Mid-City. I'd put together a business plan and was so excited to talk to him about it, but he just shut me down. He said, "Ah, man, it's rough out here for a lotta people. Good luck with that."

As I look back at our relationship, each time I had an opportunity to spread my wings, when I was offered TV hosting gigs or job opportunities, he'd find a reason to shut it down. Always by saying he'd take care of me for life.

It became abundantly evident I was going to have to figure it all out on my own, and that's what I did and that's how I'm living. I'll never make the mistake of relying on a man again. I don't like being single, but I'll take the short-lived bouts of loneliness over

DEFINITION OF DOWN

the miserable bullshit any day. I'd rather have my big happy smiling self than to be in an unhappy, twisted, fake relationship that's just for the public eye. Doesn't mean Cupid's arrow still couldn't hit me any day, but Cupid and I would have to have a nice little heart-to-heart chat first.

* * * * * *

This new chapter in my life is challenging but, man, I'm having a good time and really looking forward to seeing what lies ahead. Every week, I spar with my dear friend Corey Holcomb on our radio show, the *5150 Show*. He can be so bad and so wrong, but he is hilarious and I love keeping him in check. And he respects me and what I have to say, so it's a good fit. Corey's heading straight to the top and he's doing it his way, and he inspires me to keep doing it my way. I've gotten so much support from so many great people, and I get mad love from everybody I run into at shows. When I bump into people like Queen Latifah, Fab Five Freddy, Biz Markie, Afrika Bambaattaa, it's all love. We are all part of an amazing history, and it's still a tight knit family. I also love all my Hollywood YMCA folk. I spent four years volunteering there as a certified instructor, and one day, the manager came up to me and said, "You put in more hours than anyone here and I'm going to do something about that." The next time I saw her, she slipped a check into my hand and I've been on the payroll ever since. People like Ryan Gosling have taken my classes and you'll find Denzel Washington on the basketball courts, Flea in the free weights room and Jamie Lee Curtis bringing her grandkids to the play area. It's been such a wonderful community. My kid grew up there, and for me it's like *Cheers*, you walk in and everyone knows your name. All my clients make my day every day. Most of them only know me as Darlene, a personal trainer and a single mom. They don't know my history or my past, and I'm just judged and loved for who I am.

* * * * * *

I did not want to leave this earth without telling my story. It's a true Hip Hop love story from rags to riches, and in some people's eyes, back to rags again. But I don't have one single regret. I'll always cherish and love the Tracy I used to know. Back in the day, he was the coolest fella. It's hard for me to understand who he's become these days.

There's no doubt, though, he gave me the best thing ever: our son. And I am so grateful that I had a role in Hip Hop history, as a down broad to an amazing man.

No one can take that away from me. Like I said earlier, nowadays these ho's come and go, but I was the definition of down. Through all our good times and the struggles, I held it down and stayed down.

I hope I've inspired some of you to live true to what's in your heart because when you do, you'll have memories that will truly last a lifetime. God bless all of you, my friends and fans, for all the love you've given me over the years.

The truth is, love is a crap shoot. It ain't the end of the world if it goes south. Just hold your head up and push on.

* * * * * *

POSTSCRIPT

I was sitting in C.J.'s Cafe on Pico Blvd. in Mid-City one Sunday morning. A friend and I were having breakfast, when all of a sudden we heard some loud bumpin' bass. A man was just parking his Cadillac across the street, and you could hear that bass coming through the closed windows. All the people in the restaurant turned to see who was gonna get out of that car, and we watched as a big ol' dude opened the door. He must've been 6'4" and an easy 400 pounds. I'll never forget his shirt. It was a custom job from a swap meet with a giant photo of his girl or some girl, spread out, legs open, all exposed, like she was just putting it out there. People in the restaurant gasped when they realized what he was wearing, but you could see he was the type of dude who clearly didn't give a sheeeet what anybody thought. This big mountain of a man in a pornographic shirt walked into C.J.'s and some people were relieved when he picked up his food to go.

We watched him walk out and pass the window where I was sitting. He did a double take when he saw me, and he turned around and came back in the restaurant. My friend looked at me and whispered, "Oh my God, girl! You know him?!"

Everybody's eyes were on us. He came right up to me and said, "Are you Darlene?"

I said, "Yes."

He said, "Ice T's ex-girl?"

DEFINITION OF DOWN

I said, "Yes."

He said, "Dang girl! You should write a book! You got a story."

I told him, "Thank you! I'm working on one right now."

He said, "Alright, Queen, good, good. Peace, Queen. You take care." He shook my hand and walked outside.

He was halfway across the street when he stopped, turned around and yelled: "You know what you are, Queen? You're the definition of down!" Then he turned back toward his car, got in and loudly drove away.

I looked at my friend and said, "That's it! That's the title of my book!"

* * * * * *

Shortly before the death of my friend Teena Marie, we sat down together and wrote this song. The lyrics say it all.

DEFINITION OF DOWN

Oh, I love the rain beating on my window pane,
I'll give you all my love and keep nothing for myself,
I'll sacrifice for you and pay the price for life itself,
Unconditional, like a guy who takes the fall,
Through the fire, baby, to the limit, to the wall,

Here I am, can I be your fool?
What you want? Cuz I'll get it for you,
And I don't know what to do, Cuz I'm so in love with you,
All my empty pockets spend, Ride with you til the very end,
Telling you I'm down and then I'll do it all again,

That's the definition of down,
Baby, let's get down to Ground Zero,
That's the definition of down,
Damn, I dig you, baby, and you know,
You know, yeah, you know,

Deep down will dig for you and ask for nothing in return,
I'll give you all my specials, baby, and any time you need to burn,
I'll make it so organic, daddy, just like a stroll around the park,
Get down, like nice and easy, like shadow-boxing in the dark,

Here I am, can I be your fool?
What you want? Cuz I'll get it for you,
And I don't know what to do, Cuz I'm so in love with you,
All my empty pockets spend, Ride with you til the very end,

DEFINITION OF DOWN

Telling you I'm down and that I'll do it all again, yeah,

That's the definition of down,
Baby, let's get down to Ground Zero,
That's the definition of down, I'm 'bout to put it down, baby, you know,
You know, yeah, you know, Baby, you know, yeah, you know,

Through the fire, to the limit, to the wall, Here I come every time you call, Like the autumn leaves that fall, Never hesitate to give my all,
Through the fire, to the limit, to the wall, Here I come every time you call, Like the autumn leaves that fall, Never hesitate to give my all,
Through the fire, to the limit, to the wall, Here I come every time you call, Never hesitate to give my all,
Like the autumn leaves that fall, Through the fire, to the limit, to the wall,
Never hesitate, cuz that's my definition,

That's the definition of down (of down),
Baby, let's get down to Ground Zero (baby, let's get down),
That's the definition of down (get down),

I'm 'bout to put it down, baby, you know (baby, and you know),
That's the definition of down (that's the definition),
Baby, let's get down to Ground Zero (baby, let's get down, down),
That's the definition of down (let's get down),

Damn, I dig you baby and you know (ahhhhh)
You know (you know), yeah, you know (you know)
Baby, you know (you know), yeah, you know, you know

* * * * * *

You've heard my side of this Hip Hop love story. Now hear from Tracy, in his own words, about me. Below are excerpts from some classic magazine interviews and television shows, offering snapshots of some beautiful moments in time.

ICE T: IN HIS OWN WORDS

RAP MASTERS May 1989
Ice says he proves his love for the opposite sex "right out there where it belongs" by encouraging his wife Darlene (who so nicely decorated his first LP cover) to take part in both onstage and off-stage affairs that pertain to his career. He says proudly, "I'm in love. I've got a wife and I'm one of the few rappers who puts their woman out in front. I'm always taking pictures with Darlene, and also, I think that women find monogamy attractive. That ain't gonna stop them from liking me, they just say, 'Ice T's married, but look how good he treats Darlene. If anything ever happened, boy, I'd love to be treated the way he treats her.' A lot of girls like Darlene a lot 'cause they say, 'She stands by him and he's crazy. This woman's got control over this man!'" Ice T likes to say that it's Darlene "who holds him together."

Hip Hop CONNECTION July 1991
"The way I see it," he confides, "is that Darlene saved my life. She came along when I was kinda at a crossroads in my life. I was trying, to decide whether a life in rap or crime was better, and I was kinda losin' the battle, 'cos crime was easier and had better rewards. Darlene picked me up and convinced me of the talent I had, she told me that crime wasn't the way. So she helped me, she got a job and supported me, and handled my business…she kept me going. Darlene was the only one to believe in me at that time, and to that end, I feel that she saved my life. Nowadays, it's kinda like at the stage when Darlene doesn't have to do so much as before and now she kinda like works as my in-house model!"

DEFINITION OF DOWN

THE LATE LATE SHOW WITH TOM SNYDER April 1996

Tom: When you were starting out, you weren't too successful. But there was a lady in your life named Darlene who kind of helped to keep you on track, huh?

Ice: True. Basically, when you're out on the streets and you're hustling, to be honest, as a man you're trying to get girls, you know, and if the girls are rolling with the fast money, you're gonna chase that. When you're in high school, if the girls are chasing the athlete, you wanna play sports. In my neighborhood, the girls were chasing the drug dealers or the hustlers. When I met Darlene her attitude was different, she was just like, 'Don't worry about that, I know you got the potential to go out and make this money negatively but slow up, you wanna do music.' She went out and got a job. She worked for like 2-1/2 to 3 years while I was struggling, you know, trying. And I told her, I said, 'If I ever make it, you won't have to work.' I remember the day when we started making money and I told her she could quit her job. So now we have a little boy together. We've never been married, because we got this attitude, if it ain't broke, don't fix it. But we've been together and I think its important for especially a young guy to get the right girl early in his life, you know, that's not so materialistic, that's willing to help him. If you got somebody then... because it'd be real hard for me to meet somebody at this point, you know you can't trust them, you know? You don't know where they're coming from, but she was there when I was broke, when my car was in the shop. So you know, we're still down.

DETAILS Magazine July 1991

Ice: "I told her, 'Like, yo, I got another girlfriend living in my house. I'm trying to kick her out.' And Darlene was real cool. When we finally did hook up, I was going through a metamorphosis. I used to be on the streets making money, but back then I was trying to get over in the music business and I was really broke. The harder the times got, the more I trusted her. If I would have met her when I was rollin', I don't know if I'd trust her today. That's something else she had to deal with–being broke and being with Ice T. You still got to smile and keep on that front. Even though we were broke, she knew that I could take five minutes out and go scam 20 G's. I needed a girl who was ready to say, 'Don't do it, Ice. It's ok.' That's what made her really attractive to me. When I was trying to get my record deal, she went to work as a secretary. But it took like a year or two for me to believe that she was really down with me. All the publicity she has now she never wanted. All she wanted to do was wash the dog, cook and clean. I told Darlene early: you can either be on the inside or the outside. The outside woman leaves the room when the guys talk. The inside one gets to hear the guys talk about everything. But she has to uphold a code of silence and not go tell their girlfriends. I don't even think the girls look at Darlene as a girl, they look at her as somebody they ain't never gonna be. I tell Darlene, 'The homies, will be around forever, they'll kill for you, but these girls, they're jealous.' My boys are always saying, 'I'm looking for a Darlene.' When I go out with Darlene, I don't have to dress up. She's like jewelry."

ATLANTA JOURNAL February 9th, 1996
(Ice T played 20 questions with the news publication)
Question #7: What is the quality you most like in a woman?
Answer: Loyalty.
Question #11: What or who is the greatest love of your life?
Answer: I'm in love with Darlene. We never got married but she has dealt with me so I gotta love her the most. I don't know how long she's going to but she loves me now, I think.

RAP PAGES Magazine October 1991
"To keep your relationship together when you're a celebrity and you're married, you have to have a woman who's pretty much secure, 'cause she knows when I'm on stage I'm not only sellin' me, I'm sellin' a sexual thing to a lot of females. You have to have love and support. My wife, Darlene, has as many fans as me. If we're jealous about anything, we both gotta watch each other 'cause both of us are fly."

DEFINITION OF DOWN

BLACK BEAT Magazine April 1990

According to the M.C., these days are the best times of Ice T's life. "I've been in the situation where I thought I was living the best time of my life, with the money, the jewels and all of that from hustling. But I was nowhere as happy as I am making music, and not even having money," he says, with a glance toward another reason for his happiness, super fine main squeeze Darlene.

VOX Magazine February 1993

"Darlene. I call her my 'wife' but I don't believe in marriage. You either want to be with somebody or you don't. We'll stay together as long as we stay the same. If I start beating on you, or you start dogging on me, then it's over. I'll only love her for as long as we stay the same. I don't believe in this eternal shit. She was the girl who wanted me to have my own dreams and my own money, she pushed me and I connected with her. I wouldn't be happy with someone who wanted nothing."

SPIN Magazine 3rd Annual Swimsuit Issue 1989

(Under black & white photo of Ice & Darlene)

Question: Who would you like to be on a deserted beach with?

Darlene: Ice.

Ice T: Darlene.

PHOTOS

PG. 6 Clockwise from top left: Enjoying some poolside fun with Tracy at Caesars Palace Las Vegas. – 1988 • Hugging Jam Master Jay (RIP) after a Run DMC concert in L.A. – 1986 • Sporting my favorite blue leather jacket, makeup free. I had just wrapped my first commercial for a local optometrist to promote colored contacts that just came out that year. I received a small fee and a year's supply of colored contacts. • Ice posing on our convertible Porsche. – 1987 • Crazy Legs (Rock Steady Crew) and Tracy riding the subway on his first trip to NYC trying to get a record deal. – 1986 • At a New Music Seminar party with Doug E. Fresh, Kool Moe Dee, Just Ice, Barry Bee, Scott La Rock, KRS-One, D-Nice and Ice (Tracy). – 1987 • With my dear friend Teena Marie (RIP). – 2005

PG. 9 This was taken at my grandma's house by a traveling door-to-door photographer when I was a year old. Don't know why I'm crying, though. – 1968

PG. 11 My dad, Pete, on his Harley in Corona (my hometown). – 1978

PG. 19 A very rare photo of Rose and me during the reception at my quinceañera. The photographer made me take it. (Rose didn't want to take it, either. You can totally tell by the expression on her face.) Hey, I tried. – 1983

PG. 22 My 8th grade yearbook photo at 14 years old.

PGS. 28 & 29 Clockwise from top left: At my dad's house with two of my dogs, June and Ramey. I was 10 years old. – 1977 • Rose (my mom). – 1972 • With my dad, Pete, in my grandmother's kitchen during Christmas. – 1986 • Celebrating my 1st birthday at Grandma's house. – 1968 • Rose and my dad, Pete, getting married. – 1970 • With my Uncle Robbie Ortiz. I was two years old and he was one. – 1969 • Doing a little horseback riding with my dad. I was two years old. – 1969 • My dad, Pete, and Grandma Connie

DEFINITION OF DOWN

in the front yard of my grandparents' home. (Still there in Corona, CA.) – 1967 • Me at two years old in a red dress. • Dad and our dog June. – 1977 • At Dad's for the summer with my dog Ramey. – 1976 • My mom, Rose, several months pregnant with me, sporting a leopard print coat. – 1966 • At Dad's with my dog June. – 1977 • With cousins Shane and Mark Ortiz, Uncle Robbie and friend Efrin. – 1984

PG. 33 Hanging with Tracy in the lobby of the Marriott at Times Square during our first trip to NYC. He had just got the record deal. – 1987

PG. 39 With Tracy at World on Wheels roller skating rink in Los Angeles. – 1988

PG. 40 On one of our first dates, riding in the back seat of Evil's Cadillac. – 1985

PG. 42 In NYC, after we received some money from Tracy's first record deal. – 1987

PG. 44 A little cuddling and clowning around in our 2nd Hollywood studio apartment. – 1986

PG. 46 My first time in NYC at Rockefeller Center. (I was freezing!) – 1987

PG. 49 Hugged up tight with Tracy. – 1988

PGS. 50 & 51 Clockwise from top left: Baby girl, happy as can be, chillin' in the lobby of the Marriott at Times Square. • Tracy posing in front of a platinum album for the movie Breakin'. • B-girl for real – with my permed big hair, Reebok sneakers and stretch leggings. I had just moved in with Tracy and this was our first studio apartment on Beachwood Drive. – 1985 • Holding my pullout cassette-deck car stereo, about to get in our new red BMW 740. – 1988 • Hanging in NYC. – 1988 • Getting some sun poolside at Caesars Palace Las Vegas. – 1988 • Tracy came into some cash. And I'm still rockin' the colored contacts from my commercial. BOOM! • One of our first dates hanging with friends. Tracy took us to see Luther Vandross at the Los Angeles Sports Arena. • Tracy posing in front of the freshly painted

Crenshaw wall with the Rhyme Pays logo and all our names. – 1987 • Tracy and I hanging in the lobby of the Marriott at Times Square. – 1988 • Smooches for Tracy. – 1988 • Me with blonde hair. – 1986

PGS. 52 & 53 Clockwise from top left: Excited to use the new cordless landline phone in our 2nd studio apartment. – 1986 • Tracy helping Evil E with his turntables, rehearsing for a show. – 1986 • Tracy's first trip to NYC, posing in an abandoned lot in the Bronx outside of Islam's place. • It's Bonnie and Clyde. Ha! Posing in our unfinished convertible Porsche. – 1986 • Out on the town in NYC at the Palladium nightclub. – 1987 • A fresh paint job and wheels for our Porsche. – 1986 • Clowning around with Tracy at a graffiti exhibit in L.A. This is where I'd first meet Fab Five Freddy. – 1986 • With Redhead Kingpin in NYC. – 1988 • The happy couple posing in all white. – 1989 • Tracy out in NYC about to get the record deal. – 1986 • Standing in the middle of a Paris street with King T during our first European tour. – 1988 • Tracy about to rock the mic. – 1986

PG. 56 Leaning on Melle Mel up at Islam's place in the Bronx. – 1987

PG. 59 Rakim, Tracy and Professor Griff during the Dope Jam Tour. – 1988

PG. 63 Terminator X, Flavor Flav and Tracy during the Dope Jam Tour. – 1988

PG. 70 The single cover for "I'm Your Pusher." Photo taken by Glen E. Freidman.

PG. 77 Scuba diving in Oahu. – 1989

PGS. 78 & 79 Clockwise from top left: Shot of the crowd at World on Wheels roller skating rink in L.A. for one of 1580 KDAY's events. – 1987 • Tracy with Rammellzee in NYC. – 1987 • A view of the stage during the New Music Seminar DJ Battle competition with the Fresh Prince (Will Smith), Ice T, MC Shan and TJ Swan. – 1987 • Biz Markie onstage during the New Music Seminar MC Battle competition. – 1987 • Ice (front row center) hanging with the members of Whodini (GrandMaster Dee, Jalil and Ecstasy) along with

DEFINITION OF DOWN

fans that came to a record store promotional event. – 1986 • Melle Mel. – 1988 • At the Palladium nightclub in NYC with Rick Rubin. (There's some water damage to this photo.) – 1987 • Blue Kangol-wearing Tracy posing on our convertible Porsche. – 1987 • KRS-One, D-Nice, MC Lyte, Daddy-O (Stetsasonic), Flavor Flav and Cool V. – 1987 • When we first met Mike Tyson in the Bronx. – 1987 • My POV shot of Tracy on a panel at the New Music Seminar. – 1988 • Kool Moe Dee about to board the tour bus during the Dope Jam Tour. – 1988 • Kurtis Blow, DJ Cash Money and the Fresh Prince (Will Smith) at the New Music Seminar DJ Battle competition. – 1988 • KRS-One and D-Nice doing a show at World on Wheels roller skating rink for a 1580 KDAY event in L.A. – 1987 • Early Ice T wearing his black leather in front of our first studio apartment. – 1985 • Getting my pose on in NYC. – 1988 • Audience shot of Super Lover Cee & Casanova Rud at the New Music Seminar DJ Battle competition in NYC. – 1988

PGS. 80 & 81 Clockwise from top left: Flavor Flav hosting for the MC battles at tour. – 1988 • Professor Griff backstage during the Dope Jam Tour. – 1988. • Tracy and Donald D in the studio. – 1988 • A shot of the crowd during the New Music Seminar MC Battle competition in NYC. That's Guru (RIP) giving me the peace sign. – 1988 • Dana Dane happily posing for me at an industry party in NYC. – 1988 • Flavor Flav and Daddy-O (Stetsasonic) at the New Music Seminar MC Battle competition. They were both hosting. – 1988 • My POV shot of MC Serch at an industry party in NYC. I couldn't help but take a photo of him carrying his pullout cassette car stereo in the club. – 1988 • A shot of the crowd at a 1580 KDAY event at World on Wheels roller skating rink. – 1988 • With Tracy and Glen E. Friedman at the Palladium nightclub in NYC. This was our first time meeting him. Later, Glen would be the photographer for all our iconic album covers (Rhyme Pays, Power, OG, Rhyme Syndicate Comin' Through) and many other single covers as well. – 1987 • Chuck D on the Dope Jam Tour. – 1988 • Tracy rocking the fly white Angora Kangol at Islam's place in the Bronx. – 1987 • Too Short during the Dope Jam Tour in Oakland, CA. – 1988 • Tracy and I hugged up tight. – 1989 • Jazzy Jeff and DJ Cash Money at the New Music Seminar DJ Battle competition in NYC. – 1987 • Arriving at the London airport for our first European trip. – 1988 • The serious couple shot. – 1989 • With Dana Dane at an industry party during the New Music Seminar in NYC. – 1988 • Scott La Rock (RIP) at World on Wheels roller skating rink in L.A. for a 1580 KDAY concert event. – 1987 • Tracy, Kid Jazz, Donald D and Afrika Bambaataa hanging out in NYC. – 1989 • Scott La Rock (RIP). – Early 1987

PG. 85 Hanging out with Tracy on the set of New Jack City with Flavor Flav, George Jackson (RIP), Allen Payne, Mario Van Peebles, Wesley Snipes, Bill Nunn and two of Flavor's kids. – 1990

PG. 90 Seven months pregnant at our first home. – 1991

PGS. 98 & 99 The happy couple at an industry party in Los Angeles. (Photo by Arnold Turner.) – 1989

PGS. 102 & 103 Clockwise from top left: With Tracy and Flavor Flav. – 1988 • On the red carpet with Tracy for the MTV Video Music Awards. – 1992 • Our first trip to Australia to promote the Power album and we meet Neil Young up at the WEA offices. – 1988 • Having a great time backstage with Tracy and King T after one of his first shows overseas in Hamburg, Germany. – 1988 • Tracy (holding our son, Little Ice) and my dad, Pete, celebrating our son's 3rd birthday. – 1994 • Signing Power albums with DJ Evil E at a record store on our first promotional trip to Australia. – 1988 • A classic article from Rap Masters magazine. – 1988 • Tracy and Eric B in NYC. – 1987 • Tracy with Chuck D and Ice Cube. – 1991 • All hugged up at the House of Blues in Florida. – 1992 • Hanging with Tracy while he performed for a small crowd during our first trip to Japan. – 1988/89 • The royal couple. – 1989/90 • A handwritten birthday card from Tracy. – 1997 • On the red carpet with Tracy for the Soul Train Music Awards. – 1989 • Tracy clowning around at a record store, placing our first album (Rhyme Pays) in front of LL Cool J's. LOL. – 1987 • In Acapulco, Mexico, with Tracy on our first vacation after having our baby. – 1992 • Black and white poolside with Tracy up at the Mondrian Hotel in West Hollywood. (Peep the huge old cell phone. LOL.) – 1989 • Russell Simmons and Tracy at a pre-Grammy Awards party in NYC. – 1991 • With Divine Styler, Donald D and Tracy. – 1988

PGS. 108 & 109 A snapshot taken from the video for "I Ain't New Ta This." That's me laying down – mama came to the rescue.

PG. 113 Just chillin' with Tracy. – 1989

DEFINITION OF DOWN

PG. 134 Clockwise from left: At the Eiffel Tower on our 3rd trip to Paris for a Body Count tour. – 2000 • With MC Lyte at the opening of Hip-Hop: A Cultural Odyssey, an exhibit at the Grammy Museum in L.A. – 2011 • Visiting Grandma's house in my hometown of Corona, CA. This was our custom Porsche that Tracy helped fix up and make into a convertible – we called it "blowing the brains out" because it was a very big deal. (Ice owned a Porsche repair shop in L.A., Unique Porsche, that did the work.) • Having a little fun with Biz Markie at a Jermaine Dupri party in L.A. – 1998 • DJ Evil E (in the back) and Tracy rehearsing before a show in a Glendale, CA, nightclub. – 1986 • Hugged up backstage with Tracy after a Body Count show in Canada. – 1992 • Tracy and me. – 1996 • Our adorable son, Ice, when he was 10 years old.

PG. 135 Feeling my true b-girl roots: rocking some old school Gazelle glasses, original nameplate belt and blasting a boombox. YES! (Taken by photographer Nathan Sebakijje in L.A.) – 2012

PGS. 136 & 137 Clockwise from top left: With Method Man in L.A. – 1994 • With Snoop Dogg and Betsy. – 2001 • Kicking it with Tracy on Vine and Hollywood. – 1990 • • Hanging with some of my family while attending the 30th anniversary for Radiotron at MacArthur Park in L.A. (Cousin Johnnie and his wife, Tanya Aguilar; cousins Steve and Emilio Flores; Aunt Sandi Flores; cousins Rosana Plasencia and Ayanna Aguilar.) – 2013 • New Year's Eve with Tracy. – 1996 • With my 8-month-old son, Ice. • My sweet doggies: my pit, 187, and a puppy Mija. (May they both RIP.) • Backstage with Kid Ink after one of his local shows. I was invited to come meet this current rapper who had my Power image tattooed on him. Oh, and he also added wings to it and turned me into an angel. I call this "new school pays respect to the old school." Love it! • Having some silly photo booth fun with my son. – 1995 • With Afrika Bambaataa at Hip-Hop: A Cultural Odyssey, an exhibit at the Grammy Museum in L.A. – 2011 • Loving on my big baby boy, Ice, when he was three months old. – 1992 • Tracy and our son, Little Ice. – 2002 • With my sister JoAnn. – 2010 • Having a blast with Tracy at our girl Heidi Cuda's birthday luau in Sherman Oaks, CA. – 1998 • East and West Coast kicking it big time with Evil E, Tracy, Slick Rick, TJ Swan, GrandMaster Dee and Eazy E. – 1989 • Christmas with my aunts Sandi Flores and Teri Aguilar and my beautiful grandma Connie Ortiz. – 2014 • My first English bulldog, Chopper. And yes, he's rocking a Syndicate shirt. – 1998 • Having fun in Inglewood, CA. – 2010 • Just me, teeth and all. LOL.

THANK YOUs

Darlene and Heidi would like to thank: Paul Stewart; Susan von Seggern; the Ortiz, Flores, and Aguilar families; Aunt Sandy; the Cuda, Siegmund, and Gagnon families; Valentin "Junior" Martinez; Joann Venegas; Annalisa Mastroianni; Anoush Kirakosian; Annette Vanos; the Hollywood YMCA; Lyft; Ron Miller; Kenyetta Jeffries; Corey Holcomb; Marsha S. Miller; The Zims; Colton Simpson; Mija "Boom Boom" Ortiz; Kellie Nowell O'Reilly; Jilla St.Germain; Win Rhodes and anyone who's loaned them cash in the last two years, provided a meal or put Darlene up (no joke).

BIG THANK YOU to Glen E. Friedman for letting us use the cover and back cover shots from *Power* to put together the book cover. Eternally grateful!

BIOs

Darlene Ortiz is widely known as the first cover girl of rap. Her poses for such seminal Ice T albums as *Rhyme Pays* and *Power* made her a Hip Hop icon. She also starred in multiple music videos and modeled in dozens of magazines. She co-hosts a radio show with comedian Corey Holcomb that boasts thousand of listeners. Ortiz is a fitness instructor, songwriter and can claim acting on her resume, starring in a scene with Denzel Washington in the film *Ricochet*.

Heidi Siegmund Cuda is an Emmy Award winning producer and the author of *The Ice Opinion* with Ice T, the first book of rap. She also wrote *Got Your Back* with Tupac's bodyguard Frank Alexander; *Sublime's Brad Nowell: Crazy Fool (Portrait of a Punk)*; and *Warped Book: Tales of Freedom and Psychotic Ambition*, about the Vans Warped Tour. Cuda is a former investigative producer for *Fox 11 News* and former music critic and columnist for the *Los Angeles Times*. She now writes screenplays.

Connie Ortiz

March 7, 1924 - June 14, 2015

Another Angel in Heaven